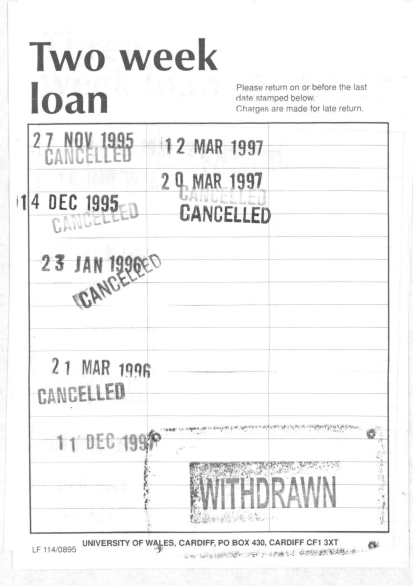

COUPLES IN CRISIS
Facing marital breakdown

by

CHRIS BELSHAW and MICHAEL STRUTT

LONDON
VICTOR GOLLANCZ LTD
1984

British Library Cataloguing in Publication Data
Belshaw, Chris
   Couples in crisis.
   1. Separation (Psychology)   2. Divorce
   I. Title   II. Strutt, Michael
   306.8'9   HQ814

   ISBN 0-575-03445-9
   ISBN 0-575-03468-8 Pbk

Phototypeset by Tradespools Limited, Frome, Somerset
Printed in Great Britain by
St Edmundsbury Press, Bury St Edmunds, Suffolk

Contents

Acknowledgements

It is only by writing a book that you appreciate all the help that is needed to produce one that is worthwhile. We thank the many people who helped us generously and with whom we were able to explore our ideas. We are particularly grateful to those who were willing to share their personal experiences. Our special thanks go to:

Rosemary Russell, who suggested improvements and encouraged us; Renate Olins and Pam Tyler both read the manuscript and offered much helpful advice; Evelyn Hunter, who guided and edited our efforts from the beginning; Maggie Belshaw, who made pertinent contributions and typed some early drafts; Desmond Biddulph read our Dynamics chapter and checked our understanding of psychology; Benedict Birnberg for checking our legal terms; John Cornwell clarified the work of a divorce solicitor; Leo Abse MP, gave us encouragement and explained the background to changing legislation; Caroline and Chris Dorling and Greta Martens for their contributions; Elizabeth Hedgecock, whose patient re-typing of our many drafts was invaluable and who made her own contributions to the book; Pat Blake for providing photocopying facilities when we most needed them.

Preface

This book is the result of a chance meeting in late 1981 which led us to meet again a few weeks later for professional reasons. As we exchanged more personal details, we discovered that aspects of our separate experiences of marriage breakdown, together with those of some people we knew, amounted to a considerable body of knowledge that we wanted to share. We decided to combine our resources and write a book in the hope that other people would benefit. This is the result.

It is very much the product of our own experience and the experience of others who have faced their marriage difficulties or worked towards amicable divorce—with the help of professionals working in this field. We did not adopt a sociological approach involving surveys, extensive interviews or questionnaires since the results are often published in a way not suited to the ordinary reader. This approach can also miss the nuances in a complex area of human relations. Rather, we have presented what we have found and what has come to us, and researched the rest. As a result we felt freer to emphasise the more productive parts of people's attempts to deal positively with difficult problems.

Sexual problems, or marriage problems among the ethnic minority communities are not discussed specifically in the book. We have felt it important to keep to our main theme though what we say will have relevance in these areas.

Where we illustrate by example, all the incidents happened with only slight changes by us of names and the occasional fact where this might identify the people involved. Some of the examples are personal ones. We explain legal terms in everyday language and provide a list of these at the end of the book.

The law, where we discuss it, applies to England and Wales. There are some distinct differences in Scotland and Northern Ireland.

The words "he or she" are often used to indicate both sexes, but to make the book more readable "he" is sometimes used alone to indicate both.

Introduction

No one needs to be told how painful divorce can be for all but a very fortunate few. Often we wish afterwards that somehow things could have worked out differently. It can be a very long time before we are able to regain our normal spirits, or be convinced that life with someone else might work.

The message of this book is that in many cases—and we hope in yours—it is not too late to do quite a lot to help yourself. We are sure that a book can help in such difficult and sensitive circumstances. A marriage breakdown need *not* slide out of control. If you are in the traumatic stage that so often precedes a break-up, there is much you can do to prevent misunderstandings from getting out of hand and to express your own upset constructively. At the same time it is possible if you divorce to create a very positive basis for staying on reasonable terms with your partner and this is particularly important where there are children. If you are already separated or divorced, there are still ways of handling the situation which can bring increased peace of mind in the long run, even if your partner will not co-operate.

What we advocate is an approach to marital breakdown which can make it easier for you to cope with the practical and emotional problems. At the same time, it can transform the relationship with your partner after divorce into a positive one for as long as you remain in touch. It involves a willingness to be patient, understanding and collected about what either of you wants. The aim is to solve problems that arise in a way which will preserve, and even build up, self-respect and care and respect for each other. You may not feel like this but couples who have made the effort—often reluctantly at first—have found that it makes life easier eventually. We don't offer a complete answer or "method" for dealing with breakdown but suggest ways of working with the situation to find your own solutions. This will enable you to consider other points of view and anticipate some problems before they arise.

Lacking the experience and practice that makes us skilful in other areas of life, we find marriage hard to handle when it goes wrong. And because it is so often traumatic, very many people can do no more than flounder through an extended period of months, even years, in which many emotions are aroused and their whole life is turned upside down. But there are skills involved which can be learned and ways of applying them which bring results. The approach that we describe in the following chapters can help you deal with anger, guilt, bitterness and a sense of loss. It may also keep you sane, and even cheerful, at times when things are black. It could also save you time and money.

But beware. Because your pride, your self-esteem, your insecurities and your ability to see life from other points of view will all be tested, it is likely to prove anything but easy to put what we have to say into practice at first. To face marital breakdown positively, as we suggest, may demand of you more patience, tact, forgiveness and forbearance than you thought you had. You may exasperate relatives, puzzle your friends and anger your partner. You may find yourself examining your motives and your relationships with others in a way you never have before. It may force even more heart-searching about what you and your mate have wanted from each other and what you want in life for yourself. And you may wonder at times— perhaps when a storm of abuse greets your attempts to communicate—whether it is all worth the bother. If you find yourself in similar difficulties in a second marriage, it is likely to be no less painful.

Throughout the industrialised world the divorce rate is climbing, partly as a result of greater social mobility and freedom. In England and Wales it is now the highest in Europe, about one in three according to government statistics.* Why this trend should affect so many societies no one is sure, but a number of reasons have been put forward. We would point to origins in the divorce peak after the Second World War—a period when greater equality was made necessary by the war effort. Also, war experiences changed people's perceptions of themselves.

* Office of Population Censuses and Surveys

Some recent American research on the subject seems to point to a close correlation between the rise in jobs for women and the increase in the divorce rate. This may be only a partial explanation, however. It could be argued that because married women are at work in greater numbers than ever before, they now have the same chance as men have always had to compare their lives with others. The women's movement has enabled women to become more independent, and it has given confidence to many who want to have careers as well as, or instead of, bringing up a family. Accordingly, they are in a much stronger position than they have ever been to judge when a marriage is empty, and so more willing and better equipped to establish a life that has more meaning for them. This is borne out in Britain by the figures, which show that more women than men are now petitioning for divorce.

The fear for people who do have to divorce is the feeling that events are outside their control, perhaps for the first time in their life. And this is brought home when they consult a solicitor and encounter the machinery which governs the legal side of ending a marriage. People feel vulnerable and unprepared in a situation in which they may already be upset, angry or very worried. This is at least being recognised by some lawyers, as an article by Gwynn Davis in a legal journal showed: "The whole tenor of matrimonial proceedings is to a large extent determined by solicitors. They are responsible for translating their clients' problems into legal terms and also advising them to the limits within which they can operate in this framework. Since the client has no point of comparison, it is difficult for him to question the way in which his situation is interpreted. The solicitor therefore has considerable control over the route that is pursued."*

Davis points out that the conflicting values in our divorce law have produced a muddle. This is because the divorce reforms of 1969 failed to get rid of the idea of one partner proving that the other is at fault in order to divorce "and this invites resentment and conflict".

In contrast, says Davis: "There has been little attempt to

* *New Law Journal*, February 27, 1982

explore the element of common ground between husband and wife or to mobilise the couple's sense of fairness, which need not cease when the marriage breaks down. Much of the blame for this imbalance has been attached to aggressive solicitors who, it is said, inflame the conflict. But solicitors are bound by the system within which they operate. The procedure is not designed to cater for the interests of the family as a whole."

In their training Britain's solicitors are given no grounding in effective techniques—of the kind used in industrial relations— which can bring two parties in dispute to some agreement. And so far there are no firm plans to provide it. If there were, couples who see their friends pitted against each other by the present aggressive system might be more willing to obtain the most co-operative settlement possible through solicitors rather than looking for the easiest way out: the postal divorce or, worse, postponing taking any action. Legislation is merely a framework to deal with the legal aspects of marriage and divorce, and preferably we should deal with the other aspects ourselves instead of allowing the legal system to take over.

Divorce is already all but unbearable for many people. A survey of 327 divorced parents by *Woman* magazine, came to this conclusion: "It was hard to find divorcees willing to be interviewed—many felt the subject was still too painful, and discrepancies suggested it was still hard for the interviewees to think straight."*

The Finer Report on one-parent families in 1974 recommended an approach to the conflicts of divorce based on conciliation which it defined as "the process of engendering commonsense, reasonableness and agreement in dealing with the consequences of estrangement." This has been taken up increasingly by individual courts where the Registrars, sometimes helped by the court welfare officers, are "embarking with the parties on the common talks of negotiating an agreed settlement... The emphasis is on early intervention, face to face contact with the parties and an active role for the mediator in interpreting, negotiating and offering possible solutions."†

* *Woman*, February 27, 1982
† *New Law Journal*, (op cit)

Considerable impetus has been given to the idea of conciliation by two innovative schemes in Bristol—the Bristol "in-court" mediation scheme, which started in 1977, and the Bristol Courts Conciliation Service which followed in 1978. Solicitors act as negotiators in both these schemes, putting their skills into finding a settlement that is acceptable to both parties. Following this start, conciliation services are developing and, we hope, will spread throughout the country.

Help of this kind, particularly where two people are not on proper speaking terms, can enable a couple to make a much-needed arrangement that allows both parties to continue with their lives in comparative stability. Another approach is the new three-day self-help courses for people who are divorcing or divorced, put on by local authority probation offices. Discussions about both the legal aspects and their own feelings help people to understand much more about what they are going through. Often the courses will change a person's attitude so that they are more ready to compromise. These ways of helping are not to be confused with reconciliation, which is where two people who have parted agree to rebuild their relationship.

The incidence of divorce on such a large scale in many countries cannot be simply the result of social change and greater affluence. In part it has to be a rejection of traditional values; in part the new consciousness engendered by the women's movement, which is changing the stereotyped relationship of man to woman and seeking the deeper meaning it represents, and other pressures such as unemployment. But in this time of transformation in society another clue was given in a Home Office Working Party Report on Marriage Guidance. It said: "The trend which can be identified is that marriage is increasingly required to serve the partners' own personal development... The more that elementary economic and material needs are satisfied, the more central does personal growth become."★

All this is making an enormous demand on marriage and it is no wonder that many marriages cannot take the strain. It is this,

★ *Marriage Matters* (Home Office 1979)

we feel, that is at the heart of marriage breakdown. Because of this, divorce itself is a complex experience which has no sense or meaning if it provides freedom only at the expense of much upset and disillusion. What it does represent is change on a personal level. Whatever else can be said about it, nearly everyone will agree that divorce represents a dramatic alteration in a person's life. Change of this sort is often regarded as disastrous but we need not take a negative view of it—change can be positive and we emphasise this throughout the book.

The circumstances surrounding breakdown and divorce always contain a message, a commentary on our ability to relate closely to another person. It is a situation which, if we allow, will provide insights into ourselves—and usually tell us something we need to know. And so it is a process which can help us learn to function more fully in everyday life.

Marriage, and living with someone, is the expression of our ability to relate in the widest sense. Relationships, if they are healthy ones, allow change and provide opportunities to develop. That is how we mature and find out about ourselves and give back to the world. Marriage and divorce have meaning only if we try to understand them in this way. For this reason the relationship with our partner rarely ends the day we separate or divorce. As when we mourn someone, feelings have to be recognised and absorbed and the attachment let go. This involves real grief for that which is lost. If there are children, the relationship in most cases has to continue at some practical level anyway and so feelings have to be understood.

There is nothing remote or vague about these ideas because it is vital that we are aware whether or not our feelings are fully dealt with. If you are angry with someone, or bitter about a divorce, you still have a strong relationship with that person—even if they are now living on the other side of the world. Your energy and emotions are being engaged in a way that is little different to when you were with them. One way or another the relationship has continued and is diverting your energies. This is why we refer throughout the book to the other person as "your partner". We argue that it is important to regard separation and divorce from the standpoint of change, and the change in the

14

relationship as part of a process in which you are freed from the past.

The idea of change being a process is one you will meet again and again in the chapters that follow and, because you are involved in the process of change, you may have to make some tough decisions. It takes courage of a particular kind to create a positive but more realistic relationship out of the ashes of the old one. It takes courage of another kind to act on the realisation that a relationship must be given up and divorce is necessary. Decisions like these are hard but they may be demanded of us if we are to learn and develop in life. The problems can be just as acute if you are not legally married; when any couple breaks up after a long period together, they face the same practical and emotional problems. In coping with this change, feelings of regret often surface and need to be accepted as one of the emotions which does recede in time if allowed to.

The strong connections between marriage and the churches raise particular pressures for those people who have to take religious views into account; either their own or others'. These links are throwing up dilemmas which even the churches have yet to resolve. The book provides a wider context for the individual to weigh the issues.

Most upsetting, perhaps, is the enormous pressure put on children when their parents break up. Because children's security is rooted in the stability of their home and the presence of their parents their world can be shattered. Parents are always parents and there are many ways in which children can be protected from the worst by two parents who are prepared to make the considerable effort it may take to show that, whatever happens, they are still loved by both. Equally, it is very easy for one or both parents, interested only in themselves, to make the situation far worse than it need be. Careless words and unfeeling actions can wreck children's confidence quite unnecessarily because, given love and reassurance, most are resilient enough to take divorce in their stride.

Sadly, the results of the *Woman* survey indicated that children are being used increasingly as pawns in their parents' disputes, with one parent turning the children against the other. A further finding was that many parents felt no need to talk to their children about either the situation or their future, believing that children do not suffer much anyway. It is here that parents have a choice and a responsibility that, we believe, ought to dictate strongly some of their actions.

The breakdown of a marriage is often talked about by marriage "experts" as if it were some kind of illness, and in a way it is. It is a period when the powerful emotional and irrational side of human nature takes over and colours everything we feel. And it is hard to explain much of what is done and said in any other terms. But more accurately it is a journey of transformation which a person can either co-operate with or ignore. Try to set aside any assumptions you may have; there are many views and myths about breakdown and divorce and you will experience it in your own way.

Breakdown and divorce are extreme yet real expressions of a deeper inner process that is going on in our lives. One which can equip us to meet life with greater maturity and in better shape than before.

CHAPTER I

Dynamics of Relationships

How we choose our partners

"I'm very glad she's marrying so promptly," said Mrs Cocks. "I do believe in girls marrying young. Of course, she's very young; only just eighteen. But it's so much easier and wiser for them to marry before they form their tastes too much, don't you think?" *The Ladies of Lydon*, Margaret Kennedy.

We choose our partners for many and varied reasons. Some are obvious. We may be attracted to someone who has similar interests or who has an attractive manner. They may dress in an interesting way, share a sense of humour which makes them fun to be with, or have a similar family background so that we feel particularly comfortable with them. Or, conversely, they may be totally different to anyone else we have ever met and this is the attraction. We might be bowled over by a person's intelligence or their talents, or there may be a closely matched religious background. Behind our choice is often self-interest in the form of security, money, position or safety. We may even choose out of pity. And, not least, sexual attraction may cut across all the differences so that nothing else seems to matter.

The reasons that make us want to be with a particular person—whether we marry or live with them or not—vary infinitely from one individual to another but somehow we mostly make a choice we feel will suit us. Of course the way we make that choice varies too, so that sometimes it seems less of a choice than we realise. We may even feel that we don't choose at all, that circumstances made us fall in love with a person to whom our destiny is linked. Or, in retrospect, we may acknowledge that family pressure to marry someone because they would be a good match, and good relations with the family depend on it, persuaded us to go along with the idea, a choice we might otherwise not have made.

Choice comes in another guise in arranged Asian marriages, where the partners are selected by the two families, and the prospective couple, who may never have met, are expected to go along with that decision. It is revealing that the reactions of the two people involved can vary from warm agreement to outright refusal, by one or both. The Asian idea that the family is in a better position to choose a partner for a son or daughter because it has more experience to judge whether it would be a good match emotionally and economically has something to be said for it. By comparison, the Western premise is that a person chooses a partner for him or herself because that is exercising individual freedom, but then they may choose badly and have to divorce. So if a Western person goes along with a family's wishes and stays married for many years, while an Asian refuses to marry his family's choice, as happens among young Asians living in Europe, then conformity or otherwise goes beyond cultural patterns.

Thus it is worth commenting here that if two people whose marriage has been arranged by Asian families can stay happily married for many years, as is often the case, then free choice— the Western criterion—is far from being necessarily as desirable as it appears.

What makes us create partnerships above and beyond culture are needs we all recognise; the need for a home, for love and affection, sexual fulfilment, and for most of us the urge to bear children. We also need emotional security and appreciation of our worth.

What has all this to do with love, which in the West is regarded as the basis of marriage? Erich Fromm says this: "To love somebody is not just a strong feeling—it is a decision, it is a judgment, it is a promise."*

It is from this starting point that we want to go on to show the drives in all of us which we believe are fundamentally responsible for the choices we make in our partners, and why our feelings and judgments change. And it is from here that we will reach our main theme.

* *The Art of Loving* (Unwin Paperbacks, 1975)

People as they really are

Most of us present a face to the world, even to those who know us intimately, which may be only a part of ourselves. We are taught to believe this is how we are: that Mary is cheerful, friendly, self-reliant; that John is moody, taciturn and stubborn; and that Uncle George is always in a dream but fun really when you get to know him. It is true that we will often go further than this and say, for example, that Mary is occasionally impatient with people and sometimes gets depressed and that John can be very forthcoming and perceptive if he is in the right mood; and that Uncle George has a way with animals that you wouldn't believe.

But somehow we still do not know the real person. How is it that Mary suddenly ran off to live with a layabout who seems to care nothing for her? What is it in John that attracts so many oddball friends when he surely isn't like that; and why did Uncle George stay forty years in his job at the Gas Board when he has so many talents?

Appearances are deceptive and we are limited by our percep-tions. Why, even the people we live with and may have married thirty years ago are baffling at times.

Psychologists and psychiatrists are still arguing about the underlying complexities and contradictions in human nature and, in the meantime, the rest of us have to do the best we can with the knowledge we have.

As individuals we vary enormously in our maturity, judg-ment, skills, aspirations and capacity to love; this is what makes the world such a diverse and fascinating place. We relate to others with whom we work, live or play in many different ways, conditioned to a great degree by our childhood experi-ences. A child from a loving family which cherishes affection, and fosters confidence and a sense of humour, is much more likely to seek a mate with similar qualities no matter how their personalities may differ, and make a relationship which will bring out the best in both. Between them, they will have a lot in reserve to deal with any difficulties. In contrast, a child who is constantly abused and put down and whose talents are denied will probably grow up suspicious and fearful. He will have little chance of making mature relationships unless he changes considerably.

Most of us are born into families which fall between these two extremes, but that doesn't make it any easier. We may have come from a home where there was both love and hatred in the air simultaneously; where one parent loved the children and the other was cold or absent. There may have been a home atmosphere where problems were shared and openly discussed, or one where everything was kept behind closed doors. Our parents may have been out-going and taught us a healthy curiosity or they may have had little to teach that would enable us to get on in the world. Somehow, we have had to learn what we could during our childhood and make the best of it when we grow up and are put to the tests of adulthood.

To some extent this makes us victims or beneficiaries of the luck of the draw but how does this help us if we have pulled a shorter straw than the others? We have within us drives and talents which are unique to each of us and these can be distorted or reinforced according to our experiences as we grow up. Most of the time we are content to let these problems lie—or at least the manifestations of them. So it is that we accept that I have a bad temper, that you are never on time, that Joe cannot hold down a job. Yet these are symptoms of the distortion we have been talking about. If Jim hasn't got a bad temper but loses it only when there is good justification, what has he got that I cannot learn? If Lucy is usually on time except when the traffic is bad, what can you learn from her? And what is it that makes Joe leave one job after another?

People are as they are. Or are they? To become an adult in the true sense is not to be faultless but to function effectively and use our talents as far as we are able. And those talents include being able to relate as successfully as we can to those near to us and those we work with.

Opportunities for Change

Far from standing still emotionally and psychologically as adults, we are sent new challenges to add to those of childhood and adolescence. This is widely recognised by many psychologists, teachers and clergy, doctors and others, but until recently was almost ignored by people at large. We prefer to feel comfortable with the idea that by the age of twenty-five or so, we have reached maturity and events in adult life such as bereavement, problems at work, problems with children, and divorce, are mostly bad luck or difficulties to be shrugged off as getting in the way of normality.

Instead, the truth is we are being challenged to learn and develop still further as adults, often more than in the emotionally turbulent teenage years.

The final test, of course, is old age and death for which, some think, our lives can be seen as a preparation.

There are many examples of people's lives being changed by difficult experiences as well as pleasant ones, and our mistakes, trials and even our illnesses all offer a way to learn and develop. To suffer without learning from the experience is to waste the experience. What is more, it can invite its recurrence and this can be seen to hold true in relationships where, for example, a woman marries or lives with two or even three men in succession who each turns out to be alcoholic, or beats her up. At a subconscious level she is repeatedly making the same choice.

Here is an example. Janet married young, at twenty-one, and had a very argumentative and sometimes violent relationship with John. They divorced ten years later and Janet is now seeing Richard. They have talked of living together but Janet, understandably perhaps, wishes to stay free for the time being, and be able to see other men. Richard resents this and has also begun turning up at her home just when he feels like it. They have had some bitter arguments about this, with Richard getting very heated about the subject of other men. Now Janet is having doubts about continuing the relationship but hopes that somehow things will resolve themselves.

At the back of her mind Janet has the feeling that Richard may well be impossible to live with even if she were faithful. This situation clearly has some of the ingredients of her marriage and the test, which may be a hard one, is either to solve the problem with Richard or accept that the relationship with him cannot work and has to be given up. If she takes neither course she may well find herself in another very argumentative partnership.

To split up from someone we have lived with for a long time may be necessary and painful, but pain itself, unwelcome though it is, is a part of life we all have to confront at one time or another. The Jesuit writer, John Powell, puts it this way:

"Pain itself is not evil, to be avoided at all costs. Pain is rather a teacher from whom we can learn much. Pain is instructing us, telling us to change, to stop doing one thing or to begin doing another, to stop thinking one way and begin thinking differently. When we refuse to listen to pain and its lessons . . . in effect we have said: 'I will not listen. I will not learn. I will not change.'"*

The events which bring change, whether painful or not, do not happen randomly. They occur, modern psychologists say, at points in our lives when change needs to occur. A therapist almost invariably finds that a person comes to him for help at some point of crisis. A relationship may have broken up or is about to, powerful dreams may have disturbed him, or a business or career collapsed. The therapist will immediately see these events as signs of change or a need for change, signalled from the person's unconscious, and help to make him aware of it.

Such change is part of the process of maturing; even if it occurs in the mid-forties or later, it is better that the person be aware of it and able to co-operate with it.

Humanistic psychologists such as C.G. Jung and Roberto Assagioli accept that events in the everyday world which affect us are outward manifestations of a process going on in the psyche. So that, for example, when we become seriously ill and are forced to stay in bed for a while, it may be that we are subconsciously giving ourselves the time to take stock of ourselves or some situation which normally we stay too busy to consider.

* *The Secret of Staying in Love* (*Argus Communications*)

The change in our lives which may be required could be a practical one, perhaps compelling the hard businessman, if he will listen, to slow down and find a vocation which will bring out his artistic qualities. Or the thoughtless person may subconsciously attract some sharp raps on the knuckles which, if he listens, will suggest that he become more sensitive to other's needs. This may seem too subtle but we readily accept the principle when it is demonstrated in a way as obvious as this: A salesman who drove everywhere recklessly in his high-powered saloon, quite clearly was heading for an awful crash, particularly when two minor collisions and a near miss made no difference to his driving style. When it came, the salesman collided head-on with another car and killed the two people in it as well as himself.

The important point we want to emphasise in this section is that we are much more complex beings than we are taught to believe and we often have less real control over our lives than we like to imagine. One reason for this is that Western upbringing and education tend to train people into roles rather than help them express their true individuality, right down to the level—as the feminists have shown—that sexual stereo-typing has poisoned the natural and healthy relationship between men and women. While the most extreme feminists almost seem to want the present bias replaced by a reverse tyranny, in which men would be in some way subservient to women, the principal point that there is an imbalance indoctri-nated into most men holds true.

It can be very difficult to disentangle roles and attitudes from what our true values and feelings might be if we were not subject to such conditioning. But being aware of it is a start.

A second reason, as C.G. Jung showed, is that we all grow up with biases in our psychological makeup which leave us incomplete, so that throughout our lives we learn to express those parts of ourselves through others. And to return to the theme of his book, this applies most particularly to the partners with whom we choose to live.

In a marriage which works well each partner can help the other express some, and perhaps many, of these qualities which our role-playing does not allow us to bring forward, because close relationships must go beyond roles to work at more than a surface, social level. A couple that is complementary in this way and are willing to cast roles aside and learn from each other can help to bring out such latent qualities. It is a joy to watch a couple who relate well act in a truly complementary way, listening to each other, helping each other along.

However, sometimes couples get together who are not complementary but are polarised. That is, each one has an over-abundance of some quality that in the other may be lying totally undeveloped. Take David and Joan who married in their twenties but argued constantly almost from the moment they met. Though they were strongly attracted to each other physically, there seemed to be nothing that they did together which could not trigger an argument. Eventually they divorced. What they discovered in the process of marriage guidance counselling was that David, primarily a thinker, functioned almost entirely through his mind and was unable to respond to Joan's feelings. And Joan, who had missed out on her education but had very strong and often uncontrolled feelings, could not relate at all to David's verbal approach to everything. Each has since had to work on their hidden, unreached function which will give them a better chance in other relationships.

This brings us to an important point we want to make in this chapter: that we are not simply mind, or feelings, or bodies. All are equally necessary vehicles for self-expression and communication. We may each have a bias towards one or another and there is nothing wrong in this but if we over-use one at the expense of the other two, we are in trouble. In John Powell's words:

"Man is not simple. He is composed of body, mind and spirit and he has needs on all three levels of his existence. He has needs and appetites that are physical, psychological and spiritual. Frustration at any one of these levels can produce agony in the whole organism."*

A diagram may help to show these three areas, which all must function so that we can operate successfully in the everyday world and also enjoy good health.

* *The Secret of Staying in Love* (op cit)

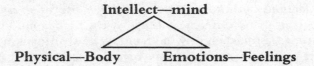

Intellect—mind

Physical—Body   Emotions—Feelings

These three sides of our nature are within all of us. By using our bodies we explore the world and become close to others; our emotions and feelings enable us to savour experience, to empathise and communicate non-verbally and our minds can put our experience into a context and help guide us. Together the three create meaning.

What's Going on in the Psyche

Any relationship between two people will involve the inter-action of the two halves of each other's psyche—the conscious and unconscious—so that in effect four people, not two, are relating to each other. The discovery of the unconscious, the submerged part of our nature over which we have no control, was made by Sigmund Freud at the turn of the century and it is among the most important discoveries of modern times.

Freud established depth psychology as a field worthy of study and his pioneering work was quickly taken up by others, including the Swiss psychiatrist C.G. Jung, who collaborated with him. However, Jung split with Freud in 1911–12 over the theory, fundamental to Freud, that sexuality and in particular fantasies of incest, are man's dominating instinct. Jung believed there were other crucial factors and, throughout the years until his death in 1961, he carried out an enormous amount of research in many fields to back his view.

The split between Jung and Freud resulted in a rift which even now divides the whole psycho-therapeutic movement, with im-plications in many areas of life and particularly mental health. We mention this for two reasons. The first is that the Freudian view of man's nature is still a predominating one, so that, with its limita-tions, it is at the basis of the popular view of what is inside our minds. The second is that Jung, in a lifetime of psycho-therapeutic work and diverse scholarship in which he studied ancient texts and religions, primitive peoples and the use of dreams and symbols in many different cultures, went far beyond Freud to produce an astonishingly wide-ranging view of mankind.

Jung's ideas form the basis of this section and, indeed, underlie much of what we have to say throughout this book. The nature of the psyche, which is the totality in which the mind operates, is a huge subject but what we will do here is summarise and simplify *some* of its aspects which are relevant to our theme. Jung's ideas are complex and subtle but we hope, in this highly selective way, to provide insights into how individuals and the relationships they make function in the way they do.

Jung's view was that modern man had become separated from the primitive instinctual side of his nature and that this split was the cause of many problems at both personal and group level, extending even to mass "illness" such as the rise of Hitler's Reich.

Jung's investigation of these separate functions led him to describe distinct ways in which individual people behave. He also showed that where we do not try consciously to integrate them, our unconscious may act for us instead. It was Jung who coined the terms "introvert" and "extrovert" which have become common usage. However, they are not generally used in the way that he meant. The popular view is that an extrovert is someone who is outgoing, plain-speaking and probably easy to get on with, while an introvert keeps to himself, is difficult to make conversation with, and thinks too much. This may be true of some people but it is a crude over-simplification of what Jung had in mind since he was really talking about the way a person experiences life. From this standpoint an extrovert is someone who is completely involved in the world about him, who tries to accept it exactly as it is even if he finds it perplexing at times. He distrusts the idea of having any profound thoughts about himself and accepts the majority view. In contrast the introvert evaluates his experience of the world and ponders on what he finds. To him the world is what he makes of it and not what at first sight it appears to be. His own thoughts are important to him and he is likely to trust them much more than he trusts accepted views.

A person tends to be predominantly introvert or predominantly extrovert but normally will combine something of the two, or he may alternate between one or the other depending on what he is doing. For example, someone who tends to be quiet and thoughtful may suddenly become the life and soul of the party after he has had a few drinks and his extrovert side takes over.

Jung also identified and classified a system of character typing which had been in use for centuries and which he called the four functions. There are four distinct ways by which we handle and judge things in everyday life. They are qualities of temperament formed in part by our experiences and in each of us one of them is likely to be more strongly developed than the others. The four functions are Thinking, Feeling, Sensation and Intuition.

The person with Thinking as his main function tends to deal with everything at a logical level. Anything for which there is no logical answer worries him and so he can be completely at sea where his feelings are concerned. The Feeling type is completely at home with his emotions and is able to tune into other people's feelings and attitudes. He dislikes logical responses to everything, being aware that life is not so cut and dried. The Sensation type has a practical, everyday awareness of all that is around him and likes routine. He also likes life to be exactly as it appears to be without questioning or debating what he knows. The person in whom Intuition is dominant operates by hunch for much of the time and seems to pluck ideas from nowhere. He can have the useful knack of spotting the essence of what needs to be done in a situation but, because he does not like routine, he tends to initiate but not follow through where a lot of work is needed.

Jung showed that the four functions work as pairs of opposites, so that Thinking and Feeling, and Sensation and Intuition, are linked. One of the functions in a pair will tend to be predominant at the expense of the other which, therefore, remains unconscious and so inaccessible until we make efforts to balance them. For example, a person who is dominated by his Thinking function may find it hard to cope in a situation where feelings are important, such as a love relationship. And a person who is Sensation dominated may be too concerned with the immediate pleasures of life at the expense of having any regard for the future.

A function which predominates can come in very useful where we use it as a special talent. For instance, the Feeling person may have considerable aptitude for working with other people, or for acting, both of which demand the ability to build up a strong rapport with others. But the less dominant function would still need to be integrated.

The importance of the concept of the four functions is that it provides in part a yardstick with which a particular person can be understood and it also helps us to understand the ways in which we may be different from them.

Jung found, through working with many patients, that another concept about ourselves which had been long known was also valid. This is the idea that each person has a masculine and feminine side to his nature. In a man the masculine instincts are usually the stronger ones and those he is in touch with. These include the qualities of drive, aggression, rational thinking and a need for goals. In a woman the feminine instincts are usually the ones she identifies with and these include the urge to nurture, receptivity to others, adaptability and thought processes which are intuitive rather than rational, though just as valid.

In a man the masculine drives are part of his conscious self while the feminine side, which Jung called the anima, is generally unconscious and needs to be integrated. The feminine in a man relates to values of gentleness, caring and feeling which have to be developed if he is to become a whole person. Similarly, the feminine values are those with which women are consciously in touch as a rule, so that it is the unconscious masculine side, which Jung called the animus, which a woman needs to develop if she is to be whole.

Jung showed that the extent to which we are in touch with this unconscious side of ourselves can make a great deal of difference in terms of the personalities of the sexual partners we are attracted to.

The present-day battle over the roles of men and women in Western society is the result of a clash between increasing awareness and the stereotyped ways in which we are still expected to conform to social norms which do not acknowledge that we have both the masculine and feminine within us. This clash is played out directly in the dissatisfactions people feel in their relationships. We all know the classic situation in childhood when a boy falls down and cuts his knee and then is told by his parents to be grown up and stop crying, while a girl to whom the same thing happens is more often picked up, comforted and allowed to cry. What both need essentially is the parent's acceptance of their pain and some comforting, thus acknowledging the child's feelings.

We tend to divide male and female roles into stereotyped sets of actions and only the most noisy protests of women's lib groups has forced the issue into the open—incidentally using women's masculine energies to do it. Even so the Peter and Jane children's reading books in Britain still perpetuate the myth by showing what boys are supposed to do, such as playing football, riding bikes and going on adventures while girls sit at home and read books, help mother with the cooking and wash dishes. The emphasis usually in these books is on the boys doing something active while the girls watch—a travesty of the masculine and feminine principles.

Most of us continue to make our relationships in marriage on these shaky foundations, full of expectations of what male and female are and are supposed to do while being unaware of the sexual polarity within each of us. But while on a superficial level this crude division seemed to work in Victorian times, with the emancipation of today feelings of anger, resentment and jealousy which build up cannot be dismissed.

How we experience life individually will depend on the combination of all these elements within us, but an important factor is the way we interrelate with others, particularly in close relationships. It is here that a very important psychological mechanism, called projection, comes into play. This is an unconscious trick of the mind by which we tend to see in others aspects of our character which we do not want to admit about ourselves. The person who is always accusing others of being difficult and argumentative is often observed to be like this himself. A graphic example is the claim by Hitler in the 1930s

29

that Churchill was a warmonger, rampaging about Europe looking for excuses to start a conflict.

Projection is something we do quite without knowing it and usually it impairs our judgment only in areas where we are vulnerable, such as particular sensitivities or things we feel very strongly about for some reason. Strong emotions are the hallmarks of projection. The best example is that of falling in love. When we fall in love we project on to the other person qualities which are ideals we hold in ourselves, perhaps that of the perfect woman or perfect man. It is when we gradually see the person as they really are, with ordinary human virtues and failings, that we withdraw the projection and have to relate to them as a real person. Sometimes this is very hard, or even impossible, to do because the real person may be very different from what we thought. When two people get down to seeing each other in this way the realisation can be so disillusioning that it may be impossible to continue the relationship.

Projection also reveals itself in other ways. Our unconscious wishes and fears can lead us into circumstances, or to people in our lives, that we least expect. Here are two examples:

A man went to a therapist to try to find out why his second marriage was in trouble. His second wife, exactly like the first, had run off to an exciting new man in another country. The therapy brought to light that a hidden and unexpected part of his nature was that of a free-loving adventurer. Being unaware of this he had acted in ways which influenced his wife and she had then acted out what was part of his own nature.

In the second example, a man spent years looking for a gentle, artistic woman with whom he could have a perfect relationship. Instead he constantly found himself with women who appeared charming but turned out to be stubborn and tyrannical. It turned out that his long-forgotten childhood experiences of women had led him always to expect the worst in them, so that at a deep subconscious level he was allowing himself to be attracted to difficult partners instead.

Very often we notice unattractive qualities in other people which in fact are aspects of our own personality which we

30

cannot acknowledge at a conscious level because they do not fit in with our image of ourselves. Projection is equally a factor in qualities we admire in someone else—they are often unexpressed qualities we have ourselves.

Another important idea used in psychology is that of repression. Something which is repressed is held in the unconscious so that we are not aware of it at a conscious level. It could be an event or events in childhood or adolescence which have been conveniently "forgotten" because they were very upsetting. Sometimes, because of the way a person has been brought up, he may repress certain feelings such as affection, tenderness and spontaneity. Most people as they grow up leave some unfortunate memories behind and it is as well that we do, but where our natural behaviour patterns are seriously modified by difficult experiences, this can have its repercussions in adult relationships.

One couple married in their early twenties, but it was not successful. Among other problems Mary found Eric unsatisfactory in a way that was a constant undercurrent during their life together, but which Eric only came to understand some time after they separated, when he was persuaded to join a yoga class which included exercises involving the pupils in holding eye contact and touching each other. He realised very quickly that compared with the other people in the class he was extremely inhibited about touching other people and, much later, realised that this inhibition had been at least partly responsible for Mary's attitude towards him. It was a year or two later that he was able to cast his mind back to his childhood and recall, for the first time, that he was constantly being punished for misdemeanors and told to "shut up". He noticed too that it was a family pattern that people rarely touched each other, or cuddled, and this was something he felt he had missed.

A variety of experiences can make us repress our normal human responses, making an indelible mark on us. War is one of them as the following example shows:

In 1981 four veterans of the Vietnam war became the first Americans to go back to the country since the pull-out by the United States in 1975. A journalist who went with them wrote:

"On the fifth day we flew south to Saigon, now Ho Chi Minh City, passing over the wasted jungles and fields of dead earth and bomb craters. As we looked down over the newly erected villages and re-cultivated rice paddies I said to Michael Harbert: Another veteran once said to me, 'I never thought of Vietnam as a country before. It was just a war.' Did you feel' like that? Harbert, who knew Vietnam only from the air, had fought a war of almost clinical detachment. 'It wasn't even that for me,' he said. 'It was just a set of co-ordinates.'"*

It is an example of how a normally sensitive man can be trained to become the calculating fighting machine that war requires.

Associated with repression is another phenomenon called rationalisation. Rationalisation is where we can find spurious reasons why we do or believe something but will not face the real reason. It allows us to take a course of action or cling to a particular idea or ideas so that we do not have to change, or accept something we do not want. Because it happens unconsciously we genuinely see something in a certain way while everyone we know may be able to see clearly that this is not so. A simple example is the person who stays in the same job long after the time they recognised they should make a move. They ignore these feelings by saying to themselves that the job is stable and secure and it would now be a "risk" to change.

Another example is the girl who wants to marry a man whom her relatives and friends are certain is not good for her. Some may even point this out but she is in love with him and cannot accept that he has any serious faults. Yes, she does know that he likes to go out drinking several nights a week and he has got into debt lately. And, yes, she felt terrible after he came home drunk a couple of times and got rough with her. But "he is a good guy at heart and will settle down when we are married". That is rationalisation. If they marry and the relationship gets much worse, so that her family have to intervene for her safety, she may then say: "I should have known what would happen." Of course, no one could have said for certain that the girl's

* *The Observer Magazine*, April 18, 1982

judgment was wrong, but she wanted things her way while they could see before the marriage that the odds were stacked against her.

Finally, the idea of the "shadow" side of the personality was introduced by Jung. The shadow is the repressed part of our nature, the unpleasant aspects of ourselves which other people can often see but we may be entirely unaware of. It is, therefore, the area where we are most sensitive to other people's criticisms and also where we are emotionally the most vulnerable. Our most sensitive areas are nearly always exposed in close relationships so that when someone steps in our shadow we tend to react strongly—but we could, instead, try to see if they have a point. We become aware of our partner's shadow when we get to know them more deeply after having fallen in love. Once we begin to see that person as they really are, with their share of the failings that all people have, we have to find a way of accepting their faults. Couples who argue a lot are usually experts at treading on each other's shadows as they catalogue each other's failings that they are untidy, that they always come in late, that they are lazy and so on. But used only as ammunition in a slanging match, this cannot solve anything.

Left unchecked, rationalisation and difficulties in dealing with the shadow can create serious communication problems. Two people who have fixed opinions and ideas about themselves may very often be unable to admit that they are wrong. Instead, they will find all the more reasons why they are right and so, instead of sharing their thoughts and differences honestly, barriers are built up between them. Many stalemate marriages are sustained by this foundation and it may take the rude shock of divorce and new relationships to force change.

However, new-found knowledge that we have of ourselves can be put to work. Once we become aware of where our responses originate, there is an opportunity to change those aspects of ourselves which are not productive. In time, unhelpful habits and attitudes can be discarded, leaving room for more useful ones to take their place.

Patterns of relationship

One of the strongest feelings we have when we fall in love is that being with the other person makes us complete. It is this which gives us the feeling that we "need" them. Our need for another person can be a very powerful one, but it says as much about our own qualities as those we admire in the person we love. It also reflects what we have experienced or failed to experience in our youth.

As we grow up we learn from our relationships with our parents, friends and relations and this enables us to develop into mature adults. But those aspects of our personality which, as a child, we have not developed—independence, self-reliance and so on—will continue to function on an immature level. Later, when we make relationships as adults, we may be attracted unconsciously to people from whom we can learn about these undeveloped areas of ourselves.

Harry was twenty-five and Kate twenty when they married. He was happy to take the traditional husband's role as the provider and leader and she was the dutiful wife, making meals and looking after the house. This worked for several years. Kate had little experience of life at large and was happy to get the attention and care of a "parent" from the willing and helpful Harry. Harry in turn felt that by building his life round doing things for Kate he was doing what a husband is supposed to do. However, he really wanted to try new interests, travel and lead a lively social life and he felt that Kate blocked many of his ideas like a stubborn child, always complaining how bored she was. They survived an affair by Harry, when he came to the conclusion that a mutual exchange of ideas together with a sharing of sexual expression was missing from the marriage. However, he doggedly did not act on this conviction but continued to try to be the "good husband and father" since they now also had a child. Kate gradually realised too that this was not the relationship she wanted and embarked on an affair herself. Now she was asserting some of the independence she previously had lacked and Harry's continuing efforts to please her only resulted in his being pushed further and further away.

When, after Kate's affair had lasted for three years it became clear to Harry that things were not going to change, they agreed to divorce.

The real person is often behind the person you fall in love with—the one we cannot see when we are in love—and it may take a relationship as close and committed as marriage to bring out the real person in both partners. It is a process which could take two years or twenty depending on their level of maturity to start with and what lies dormant within them. Again, it will also depend on their circumstances and the nature of their relationship if and when this is triggered off. Sometimes it never happens.

Two people in a close relationship can influence each other in subtle and positive ways, so that each can learn from the other and develop those aspects which still need to mature. This is one of the hallmarks of a successful relationship whether it lasts a lifetime or not. Through living together the partners can each learn behaviour patterns that are outside their own experience and so become a more complete person—complete in the sense that Jung meant when he talked about wholeness. Dr Paul Tournier, another Swiss psychiatrist, put it another way when he said: "No one can develop freely in this world and find a full life without feeling understood by one person."*

We search for this completeness throughout relationships but there are limits. Where two people come together who are reasonably evenly developed they are likely to have a complementary relationship with the give and take this involves. It can be successful for a long time. But if, instead, they are polarised psychologically, then they may be too different from each other for the relationship to hold together. A very powerful attraction between two people is usually of this kind. Each falls under the spell of their partner because strongly undeveloped aspects of their own personality are strongly developed in the other person. The mutual attraction may be so magnetic that they cannot live without each other and find it impossible to part even when it is the only solution to conflict and violence, because each feels only half a person without the

* From *Why Am I Afraid to Tell You Who I Am?* by John Powell (Fontana Paperbacks, 1975).

other. This is often the basis of the tragic love stories you read about in the newspapers.

Far less extreme than this is the love affair of Madge, a business consultant, and Jim, a minicab driver, who met on holiday. They fell for each other almost instantly and decided to live together but quickly found themselves having rows about each others' behaviour. Madge, a strong-minded decision-maker with a lot of energy, resented what she saw as Jim's laziness. He seemed to her to not want to make any decisions affecting their life together and did little but sit around when he was not at work.

Jim, on the other hand, found Madge bossy and pushy. When she wasn't making decisions for both of them she seemed to be planning useful things for him to do. The rows got worse until, eventually, they had marriage guidance help through Jim's doctor. In fact they were so different from each other that they were hardly able to relate to each other at all at an everyday domestic level until some months after they began talking things through. Madge's drive and strong-mindedness left her unable to relax and allow Jim responsibility—and simply let him be himself. Jim, though, had been taking no responsibility, making no decisions and doing nothing outside his job. To stay together they had to meet each other half way and both gradually began to change as a result.

Another aspect of their relationship worth mentioning is that Madge was acting as a "parent" to Jim, in the way that Harry did for Kate, a sure way to create resentment sooner or later.

We find ourselves in these situations as adults because of the view we have of ourselves. It is easy to grow up adopting fixed values and ideas of who we are and it is only when these are challenged that we are likely to change. Marriage is one of the strongest challenges because, generally speaking, men and women react differently to change. Men generally do not learn how to go through changes because they do not have the same experience as women.

A girl changes to a woman as she reaches child-bearing age. If she marries she changes her name and then may become a mother. When her children grow up her role as a mother essentially disappears, then she must change again.

The woman tends to learn about change and, with her intuitive nature she is emotionally more flexible than a man who may never change after reaching puberty. He may never even notice the changes she goes through. Instead, a man often remains static emotionally and does not grow and mature. This often results in the woman growing ahead emotionally and intellectually, leaving the man behind in the process to the point that she may literally leave because she can no longer relate to him. Men being outgrown by their wives will often use blocking tactics, not questioning why things have changed between them, nor wanting to find out about themselves or what is going on. Instead, they may blame the woman and other people around, or just switch off.

These differences take us back to the masculine–feminine polarities in both men and women discussed in the last section. A woman enters a relationship with expectations of masculine qualities while the man has feminine expectations of the woman. At the same time the inner feminine quality in the man reacts with the woman and the woman's inner masculine quality reacts with the man. This helps to affirm the sense of self in both of them. However, each communicates differently. Because she usually functions at an intuitive feeling level, the woman essentially expects the man to understand her without having to put her feelings into words. To her, many areas of life are implicit. But he is mystified by her behaviour because he needs things to be made explicit. He expects her to be logical and rational but she does not function only in that way. If they each cannot use their masculine and feminine qualities appropriately *on both sides* they will be at cross purposes and clash.

It is only in relationships with the opposite sex that a balance of these qualities in each individual can be achieved. This begins in childhood in relationships with parents and other adults, then continues with living together or marriage when people become adult. If two people have not achieved a reasonable balance separately before marriage then their differences may lead to a breakdown.

A further complication arises if, as sometimes happens, the

roles of a particular couple are reversed so that the woman has more masculine energy than the man and the man is functioning mainly through his feminine energy. This was one of the problems facing Madge and Jim. It was very difficult for Madge to accept that she had a very strong personality compared with Jim and that he had gentle qualities that she was inclined to overlook and could learn from. Equally, it was hard for Jim not to feel emasculated by Madge and also to accept that there were aspects of masculine behaviour that he could learn from Madge.

The only way that the personality differences which couples meet can be dealt with constructively is for each to learn from the other. It takes a willingness to communicate, to share thoughts and feelings—even at the risk of appearing ridiculous. And it demands a willingness to learn something more about yourself.

Getting Away from Stereotypes

Every person is unique but part of the puzzle of that uniqueness, and therefore ourselves, is understanding who we are underneath the layers of conditioning by parents, school and the world at large. To be sure of and pleased with our true identity is the biggest step towards relating well to others and making partnerships which work.

Certainly this has a lot to do with individuality, and some people clearly are more individualistic than others. Someone, for example, who has a strong, definite character can be seen to act in ways which mark them out as different from others despite the pressure to conform. But is this enough? How "different" is being different and how "conformist" is someone who conforms?

Let's take an example. Someone who has not conformed and has shown these characteristics through her individuality is the American actress Katherine Hepburn. Born in 1907, she was one of six children of a rich and progressive East Coast family but which lived in a community that was very conservative. A recent newspaper article, in describing her background, explained that the parents encouraged the children to express themselves and speak their minds from an early age.

Dr Hepburn (her father) believed in physical exercise as a life force and Katherine was doing acrobatics and swinging on trapeze as a child. At school she was an all-round athlete, as well as a swimmer, diver and even a figure skater. "If there was a race, I always wanted to be first. I really was not brought up to feel that women were under-dogs. I was totally unaware that we were the second-rate sex."★

Her early career in Hollywood was controversial, and the actress, who all her life has never suffered fools, frequently engaged in newsworthy battles with directors and producers.

Hepburn made her name with her very first film, *A Bill of Divorcement*, in 1932 and, says the article, George Cukor who directed it "admired the way she brought her fine intelligence to the performance, triumphing over her inexperience in film technique".

So, in her twenties, Miss Hepburn demonstrated many of the qualities that reveal a mature, well-adjusted person in charge of her own life. These qualities continued to be put to good use in a legendary film career and relationship with Spencer Tracey spanning decades during which, unlike many other stars, she kept her feet firmly on the ground. As the article notes: "She has always cherished her privacy, keeping her home life as far away from her career as possible. . . Hard tussles with illness have not diminished her enthusiasm for energetic sports such as tennis and sailing and her conquering of Parkinson's disease is as much due to her ruggedness and singleminded refusal to be crippled as expert medical care."

Katherine Hepburn is what the psychologist Abraham Maslow would call a self-actualising person: that is someone who is creative in the wide sense, has a vocation and is goal-oriented and able to maintain a productive relationship with others. Maslow maintains that some of the most-loved people in history displayed these characteristics and Miss Hepburn certainly has been loved. She is also, you will notice, very well

★ *Sunday Times Magazine*, February 7, 1982

in touch with the masculine principle of her psyche, that is she has a good deal of drive and ability to dictate events when she has a mind to.

Of course, you may say, it helps to come from a wealthy, progressive family, and that is true. It does confer advantages in life so that a person has a greater ease in succeeding in the world. But the "active principles" which Miss Hepburn shows hold true for everyone. It's a matter of gaining access to them.

Maslow maintains that all self-actualising people achieve success in many areas of their lives though they don't necessarily become famous. What they are doing is becoming uniquely themselves.

Unconventionality itself isn't uniqueness. The trick is to reach those true qualities we all have but which, in many of us, are obscured or blocked as we grow up. Being different isn't enough because it is easy, then, to fall unawares into behaving in ways which merely react against conventionality and so exchange one form of behaviour for another.

To return to Jung briefly, we find that stereotyped behaviour, whether conventional or unconventional, can spring from psychological archetypes, so that what appears unconventional on the surface can be, more accurately, merely another kind of behaviour pattern. Marie-Louise von Franz, a collaborator of Jung's, devotes a whole book to one particular archetype, the *Puer aeternus*. This is the eternal youth, someone in whom "all those characteristics that are normal in a youth of 17 or 18 are continued in later life, coupled in most cases with a strong dependence on the mother".

The eternal youth is the man who has not grown up and will try at almost any cost to avoid any responsibility as an adult. Accordingly, he is likely to go in and out of relationships, or not take marriage seriously, and be unable to cope with any kind of humdrum work. More explicitly, Marie-Louise von Franz says of him: "The typical disturbances of a man who has an outstanding mother complex are, as Jung points out, homosexuality and Don Juanism... There is always the fear of being caught in a situation from which it may be impossible to slip out again. At the same time, there is something highly symbolic—namely a fascination for dangerous sports, particularly flying and mountaineering—so as to get as high as possible, the symbolism of which is to get away from mother: that is from the earth, from ordinary life."*

We tend to see our personality in simple terms when we are really very complex with many different and contrasting facets of character. The more we discover about ourselves, the more enriched and full our life can be. Many things in life can be seen as a way by which nature gives us feedback about ourselves and who we are. These include the work we do, exercise and sport, dance and theatre and the arts generally. Illness and religious practices have this meaning as do yoga and dreams properly interpreted. One of the great teachers is relationships with others; our need for them with all that it brings makes a constant comment on our uniqueness.

* *Puer Aeternus*, Marie-Louise von Franz (Sigo Press)

CHAPTER 2

Changes in Marriage

The symbol for crisis in written Chinese is represented by the two-part character "danger" and "opportunity"—an apt description of some periods in any marriage. The top part of the character means "closing down" which could be interpreted as not facing a situation and dealing with it; the bottom half means "opening out", thus using the opportunity to develop as individuals.

Every close relationship we experience from the time we are born teaches us something about ourselves. The intimacy of marriage with its long-term commitment is a vehicle for personal change and the exchange of love. But where the marriage tie itself takes over from this process, then many of the influences to do with personal values, how to live and love and achieve our own potential, may be blocked. Marriage is essentially about both relating to another person and being yourself. In their book about self-assertion Herbert Fensterheim and Jean Baer put it this way:

"In the ideal close relationship, you establish a communion with another human being where feelings come first and you cannot separate giving and taking. In the optimal close relationship, the other person is like part of yourself. In fulfilling the other person's needs as if they were your own, you satisfy your own needs. Yet, you remain yourself as an individual. Thus both husband and wife are led to deeper, richer experiences and in the merging the individuality of each becomes stronger."*

Being able to state your own needs, and understand your partner's, is fundamental to close relationships. The quality of a particular marriage makes a clear comment on a couple's ability as individuals to relate and yet be themselves.

Most of us take into marriage a complex mixture of values, feelings, hopes and desires. They originate in our upbringing, in our education and in those ideas which we have absorbed from

* *Don't Say Yes When You Want To Say No* (Futura Paperbacks)

society at large, for example through television, newspapers and the people around us. Yet few of us can easily cope for long with a commitment of this kind at the age we choose to— usually in the twenties. Instead we carry into marriage a hotchpotch of feelings and ideas about how to live with someone and what we expect; love, happiness, security, status, the companionship found in a stable relationship and, for most of us, a partner with whom we feel committed enough to have children.

These powerful ideas which in some measure cater for important needs may, at the same time, cut across the unconscious yet vital needs of two individuals; the psychological and almost biological urge to change and develop throughout adult life. The maturing has to continue during a close relationship such as marriage; indeed it is a function of it, as we explained in the previous chapter on the dynamics of relationships. It is no wonder then that every age of marriage has its hazards.

The vital needs we are talking about, and which marriage ideally confirms, include having someone to love, acceptance of ourselves as we really are by our partners, reflection back of our uniqueness, and confirmation of our worth. Marriage has to include an awful lot and it is no wonder that marriages often do not last. It can be very difficult for partners to give to each other freely at this level if their responses are cluttered by inflexible ideas of what marriage is about, stemming from unhelpful personality traits and learned social attitudes. For example, couples who view marriage primarily as doing the right thing by society are likely to act in rigid and stereotyped ways which will become inadequate if either partner begins to change. This change for an individual can be particularly threatening when views of marriage are linked to strong cultural or religious ideas. The guilty feelings which are generated due to the conflict of emerging new attitudes and values in contrast to the old can be very destructive. They often lead, for example, to illness which, as we discuss in the chapter on Professionals, is often a symptom of a relationship in trouble. That many people's marriage problems can be seen to relate to strict doctrines of the various churches in society is becoming less relevant now with more flexible attitudes developing. It is to be remembered that although the churches and their ministers are often perceived as authoritarian, rigid, or even irrelevant, there are many understanding people within them.

The marriage service contains promises of a lifetime's commitment and is also a public statement of this to the world. However, before this seal of approval is given the churches often don't discuss fully with the couples what commitment they are really entering. How often do we see the spiritual world of the church and its values as irrelevant to the demands of everyday life—something which needs to be followed just for the "day" and then forgotten about in our daily lives? As families we may encourage this ceremony (if we are totally honest with ourselves) to fill our need for the sense of occasion it provides and for "doing the right thing".

In close-knit religious families the sense of commitment is more likely to be carried through in everyday life. Yet the aim for *all* is marriage experienced in a deep and lasting way, in the true sense of caring deeply for another person as much as for ourselves.

Increased awareness of how old values and attitudes are linked to marriage breakdown has provoked a great deal of work in the last few decades by psychologists, marriage counsellors and feminists, leading to a revolution in the state of marriage. The divorce rates alone reveal how many people are experiencing these changes. They feel helpless as the emotions and ideals which have spurred them into marriage seem insufficient to sustain it, which makes them examine their personal values and seek a code by which to live. Couples are forced by circumstances to look at the underlying realities of their own marriage sooner or later, often to find that longstanding assumptions are contradicted.

The ways in which these assumptions handicap a relationship were spelled out in the early 1970s in a famous book, *Open Marriage*, by a husband and wife anthropological team, Nena and George O'Neill.* They crystallised the problem by showing that couples, and particularly conventional couples, tend to

* *Open Marriage*, Nena and George O'Neill (Peter Owen).

44

enter marriage by unconsciously creating a rigid framework of unwritten rules which governs their behaviour and subtly blocks their development as individuals. The O'Neills called this framework the Closed Marriage Contract and showed that these unwritten rules are clauses in the contract.

The clauses or conditions they listed are: possession and ownership of the mate; sacrificing one's individual identity; always acting as a couple; adopting rigid "male" and "female" roles and insisting on absolute fidelity by coercion. This tacit agreement, the O'Neills said, results in "cutting you off not only from the outside world but from your natural desires".

Despite the suggestion implied in the book's title, *Open Marriage* does not encourage irresponsible free-living relationships for every couple in which any married person should do as they please. Instead it shows ways in which people can live more fully and face some of the more intricate responsibilities of marriage and similar relationships. Paramount is the idea of true companionship and the willingness of both partners to give each other the emotional space to develop and be themselves.

Another key book of the last two decades which has influenced many people's attitudes to contemporary marriage is Betty Friedan's *The Feminine Mystique*.* Written in the 1960s shortly before *Open Marriage*, it revealed the emptiness of many women's lives in traditional marriages in the United States—and struck a powerful chord in Europe. It described husbands and wives both trapped within stereotyped male and female roles, their creativity stifled. The book showed that many women needed, as much as men, to make some mark in the outside world and that, by being brainwashed into staying in the kitchen by advertising and the attitudes of society, they had in effect been robbed of their talents and sense of identity. Now, in her book *The Second Stage*,† Betty Friedan is advocating a path that brings a new twist to the problem: that women need to find a way to make both their mark in the world *and* fulfil their needs as homemakers—in other words to integrate their masculine and feminine nature, and that men must do the same.

* *The Feminine Mystique*, Betty Friedan (Penguin Books)
† *The Second Stage*, Betty Friedan (Michael Joseph)

A great number of marriages in both Europe and the United States founder after only about three years. Why should this be? The feelings of disappointment and failure, coming so soon after the many high hopes, are saying something fundamental about a couple's ability to adapt to the demands of a close and committed relationship, in particular one where all that they have is legally shared.

We tend to underestimate, or even disregard, these demands because we may not even be aware that they exist. Yet lacking maturity, knowledge and the behaviour skills necessary to live in an intimate relationship with someone, may make it impossible for a couple to cross the important threshold from romantic love to dealing with the challenges of day-to-day living.

Once we find that as well as virtues, our partner has common failings and irritating habits, we become disappointed. The image we have of them is flawed and their habits can take over in our imagination as the most important things we see. It is at this point in any relationship—which may occur within a few weeks or some years—that the deeper relationship really begins; and here that two people, to live amicably together, need to take account of each other's sensitivities.

One person's habits such as, for example, dropping clothes on the floor, stubbing out a cigarette end on a plate, or not giving clear answers to questions, can quickly lead to disenchantment. Increasing resentment may build up an underlying atmosphere over a long period and, if these differences remain unchecked, communication may fail altogether. Rows, accusations, long silences and similar unhelpful behaviour which becomes habitual, may also establish the beginnings of a breakdown in communication and snowball into divorce. The only way forward is to express the underlying feelings and objections so that some resolution can be found or accommodation made. By this we don't mean nagging but honest discussion about respective needs in which each partner says how they feel.

Marriage demands adaptation and a fundamental change of behaviour for most people. A sticking point can arise from an unwillingness to make the emotional move from being a single person to sharing as a couple. Jack Dominian, in his book *Marital Breakdown*★ points out that a reasonable degree of emotional maturity has to be achieved through a natural separation from the parents' influence if a person is to make a success of marriage. And he says: "The failure to achieve a minimum of emotional independence from the parents is one of the main causes of marital breakdown."

Having grown past this point of early change, which may cause little problem for many couples, marriage then requires that both partners explore themselves as a couple *and individually*. This is part of the process of continuous personal development we have talked about, and it provides the basis of intimate communication. Such intimacy goes far beyond the cosy togetherness and sexual success we are taught is the basis of marriage. As Nena and George O'Neill put it: "Love and cosiness, deeper emotional feelings, honest and open revelations, are seldom shared by husband and wife. By cutting themselves off from all possibilities of growth, they cut themselves off from their potential selves, and finally from one another."†

The most profound change during marriage is the birth of the first child. It changes everything. The balance of a couple's relationship alters irrevocably and they have to assume new roles for which emotionally it is almost impossible to prepare. Even the most competent people can flounder, but the effect on many marriages is devastating.

Most of all, this affects the woman. Vivienne Welburn in her book *Postnatal Depression*,‡ points out that birth in modern hospitals, where the high-technology approach frequently includes induction, effectively robs a mother of her control of an essentially creative act. Even worse, she is separated from her family, friends and younger children and left to "share the most private and personal of all experiences with strangers". This lowers her self-esteem and can trigger depression. Although more men are now present at their children's birth, this cannot

★ *Marital Breakdown*, Jack Dominian (Pelican)
† *Open Marriage*, Nena and George O'Neill (Peter Owen)
‡ *Postnatal Depression*, Vivienne Welburn (Fontana)

compensate for the experience a woman may have in such an impersonal system.

The full significance of being parents emerges when the baby is taken home. As Vivienne Welburn says: "There is nothing in the traditional male role which helps a man to cope with the nurturing his wife needs while she is nurturing their baby. Men expect to receive care, not give it." She reports, for example, that few men notice if their wife is becoming depressed though they are in the best position to do so. If the depression continues and a pattern becomes established it can undermine the marriage.

Growing children make huge demands on their parents' time which makes it extremely difficult to find the time that they need to share with each other. An important aspect of being together is being apart, in the sense of allowing some time and space for themselves as individuals. This involves a need to do some activity purely for oneself and without the partner. Simple yet important ways in which many people do this include quietly reading in the same room as their partner, visiting friends alone or even taking a long, peaceful soak in the bath. More clear-cut ways include taking a regular evening class, spending a few days away from home or taking a separate holiday.

The failure to create one's own space can have serious consequences, particularly for women, as Jeannette Kupfermann says in *The Ms Taken Body*★ "Depression as a bid for space and sanctuary has, as yet, gone unrecognised by psychiatrists. . . Do women innately recognise the need they have for periodic sanctuary to aid both physical and spiritual readjustment?"

The continuing pressures on women to run a home and family make it especially difficult for them to find this space, particularly during the childbearing years, while most men at least can quietly read the paper and many automatically follow an interest or hobby outside the home. Yet everybody has to have this space for their own well-being. One psychologist recently pointed out that "the need for privacy is universal" and that privacy is one of the hardest things to ask for without offering rejection.†

★ *The Ms Taken Body*, Jeannette Kupfermann (Granada)
† Talking Point, *Evening Standard*, November 30, 1982

The commitment of marriage with the ties and natural restrictions that this involves forces many people to take a hard look at their situation sooner or later. In the late twenties and around the age of thirty we may feel a sense of unease. A person may be established in a career or comfortably married, often both, or perfectly happy to remain unattached, but in some way this may no longer be enough so that our certainties no longer sustain us. We may question our marriage or job, or perhaps find ourselves taking a lover. Circumstances can focus our attention in ways which show that we have been living with a false sense of security. A common fear of people in their late twenties is that life holds little for them after thirty and some single people suddenly marry about then, having felt increasingly that life was passing them by.

Dissatisfaction which builds up during the thirties may emerge as deep conflict at a time when a home is well established and children, if there are any, are probably at school. There is more scope for one or both partners to reflect on the differences between them. These can surface, for example, as boredom and a lack of spark in the relationship which may be drifting. One ex-husband said: "Although we hardly ever went out, whenever I suggested that we did something interesting or different together, Jenny rarely responded. After a while I felt I was being blocked—as if a wall was being built up in front of me month by month."

At this time too, personality differences which may not have mattered before can become polarised so that two people's needs feed each other in a destructive way, creating a pattern which will dominate their everyday life. For example, the over-helpful wife who waits on her idle husband, and the man who dominates every conversation while the woman is content to say little, may find in the end that each dislikes the other for it. What was an unconscious collusion at first develops into resentment and anger that the other partner is acting in that way when each needs to behave differently.

The time around forty is another period when many people feel unsettled in marriage and sometimes make sudden changes. Often dubbed the "mid-life crisis" this is the realisation that the youthful years have gone and old age, as they see it, is all that lies ahead. This is why it is not unusual for men and women reaching their forties to become disillusioned with their life, or kick against a long-standing marriage by becoming involved with someone much younger.

A compelling urge for some people in their forties is to make a positive change and sometimes they may give up their job and embark on a completely new career or lifestyle. Sometimes a person realises that they need to make a complete re-evaluation deep within themselves and a big change can be part of carrying this out. Where a relationship needs to change and develop at this point, a couple can use the opportunity to work through these problems. In this way they can avoid burning too many boats and becoming victims of the situation.

However, the "mid-life" crisis goes far deeper than simply changing partners, finding a new career or coping with the menopause. Everybody has an unconventional side somewhere in their nature. If that remains completely suppressed as an adult it can burst out in ways which cut across the values you hold at the time. This may be difficult to handle. We believe the middle years are not a stage you merely "get through" but are more concerned with the process of maturing. It is at this time that the attitudes and experiences of the past gathered together shape the individual's attitude to the future. This can be a period of subtle changes in which, ideally, a more measured view is reached and wisdom grows.

The physical changes in both sexes have, as people grow older, to be acknowledged but the easy acceptance, for example, that poorer health is now "normal" is, we believe, a way of giving up, an attitude of mind which interferes with the maturing process. Exercise and countless yoga and nutrition courses, among others, teach people to think about themselves and stay fit and youthful. This helps them remain physically and emotionally well and able to adapt as they grow older.

However, other people who have more fixed ideas about ageing often run into health and other problems which are reflected in the marriage relationship. These can be traced through to a lack of communication at a feeling level and also to one or both partners' difficulties in coming to terms with their identity—who they are now and what they want to do with the rest of their lives.

The middle and later years of marriage, when the children are usually striking out on their own, can be the richest for a couple who continue to relate closely. Their ability to change in step with each other makes drastic change, such as running off with a younger person, less necessary to their own development. Social norms are no longer necessarily keeping couples married in the later years when the situation for one or both is clearly deteriorating. Boredom and dissatisfaction are nowadays no less likely to lead to divorce in the fifties and beyond than at an earlier age.

As we have shown, one of the keys to a growing marriage is for each partner to be able to spend time apart from the other, for themselves, without being rejected. One factor which distinguishes some men's pastimes is that they are a recognised way for a husband to spend time quietly by himself. Fishing is an example. Until women collectively became more assertive, there was little recognition that they too need their own outlets. But this still leaves the problem of relating and true sharing to be resolved by each person, through understanding their own and their partner's needs.

CHAPTER 3

Unhappy Marriage

Most long-term relationships fall into patterns of one kind or another. It is necessary to step back periodically to see if any changes need to be made to maintain a close understanding. For couples who divorce this hardly ever happens: instead, when things start to go wrong, closeness and intimacy may slip into off-handedness. Couples can become distant, argumentative or even violent. As time passes unresolved sources of friction assume more and more importance, or else a couple become passing strangers in their own home.

Feelings of boredom, tiredness and listlessness are among the first indications of marriage difficulties but they are subtle ones since they can equally indicate temporary fatigue or other problems, perhaps at work or elsewhere in the family.

Other danger signs indicating a restlessness with the relationship that suggest underlying disharmony may be signified by a change of habits in one or both partners. Things you have put up with may now become irritating so that even simple actions, like your partner leaving clothes lying around the bedroom, or carelessly slamming doors, become wearing and set you on edge. In another situation you may find that you have gradually taken a dislike to your partner, apparently for no reason, and don't know how to deal with it. Or it may be that one of you increasingly gets home late, or works away from home more often so that the normal pattern of relating slips away.

The sense of disappointment that this generates brings many people up short. Feelings of dismay, puzzlement and even anger may intrude upon your thoughts while you go about your daily tasks—at home, at work or while you relax. These feelings may affect you for some time before you realise it.

A wife of fifteen years said: "When things changed between us it reached the point when I would drive home and sit outside in the car for half-an-hour before I could bring myself to go into the house." Every circumstance of this kind, if unchecked, may

lead to irreversible breakdown. Feelings may be disjointed so
that the situation becomes confused and uneasy and you may
feel puzzled at something in the atmosphere which you probably ignore or try to shrug off at first. Gradually these feelings
keep returning until you cannot ignore them, and you are likely
then to try to understand what is happening. It may be that you
begin noticing things which are wrong in other people's
marriages and start making comparisons with your own. Some
people compare notes with close friends, though this is more
common among women who, as a matter of course, spend more
time discussing their personal lives with each other than men.

On the other hand divorce for some gradually becomes a
reality after years of argument or other difficult behaviour such
as heavy drinking, violence, gambling or persistent affairs. It
may be a very long time before someone realises and accepts the
hopelessness of situations like these and then suddenly they
resolve to take the first steps towards divorce. This new attitude
may also show in the sentiment that "they are no longer the
person I married" or "I am no longer the person my partner
married".

The build-up of all these feelings may occur over years when
a difficult or unpleasant marriage is accepted as normal, yet they
finally crystallise into the realisation that "marriage is not
supposed to be like this".

Two common ideas are paramount for most people here: that
they have made a mistake by marrying the wrong person and
the belief that they have failed.

The break up of a marriage and family is a failure in simple
terms but beyond this may be deeper contributing factors which
could have been working away for a very long time—even from
the beginning. Often a person will gradually realise that the
feelings of closeness with their partner were only a mirage; that
there was a lack of true relationship and real feelings were not
exchanged. In *Don't Say Yes When You Want To Say No*,
Fensterheim and Baer point out that "Many husbands and wives
fail to achieve closeness in marriage because they hide behind
the iron curtain of their public selves, and don't disclose their
true feelings. They also, in ways both obvious and subtle, make

it difficult for their partners to be open, getting upset when their partners speak freely and combating openness with verbal hits and hurts, or simply withdrawing from it into a closed shell. This sets up a joint spiral of increasing falseness."*

There are marriages whose serious differences can be settled and a new understanding reached; where to break up would be to throw away too much that is worthwhile. The journalist Katherine Whitehorn says that a common misunderstanding is "If things get bad, they'll never get better again; as if the relationship were a flame that had blown out, not a fire that might need stoking." Flexible attitudes make for successful marriages and, as Miss Whitehorn adds: "Any number of variations are possible—but only if people have the guts and courage to stick with the situation and re-negotiate the contract if necessary."†

In this age of "easy divorce" it is simple to begin proceedings impulsively and the more people divorce, the more other couples may see divorce as the solution to their problems. And yet there must be many marriages that are essentially worthwhile and could be successful if the problems were worked through. It often happens, though, we believe, that even if a marriage has been successful, it reaches a point where it cannot continue if the two people involved are to develop as individuals and live fulfilling lives.

One person will usually recognise first that, as a couple, they have grown apart and feel that *their own* needs have changed. Because this does not deny that the marriage has been successful up to that point, it may be very hard for the other person to understand the nature of this change. The task in this event is for both to accept that this is so if the rift is too great to be resolved and, second, to prepare to make the break in the most caring and considerate way. It may require counselling to come to terms with the situation in either case, especially where children are involved because they will need two parents who can co-operate for their sake.

* *Don't Say Yes When You Want to Say No*, Herbert Fensterheim and Jean Baer (Futura)
† *Good Housekeeping*, November, 1982

The enormous strains of bringing up children test the parents' ability to adapt. No longer only a couple, the two partners have to try to maintain their own relationship while coping with the disruption and sheer hard work that accompanies the joys of bringing up children. A wife becomes a mother and the husband a father, roles which produce unwritten rules of behaviour that subtly create a divide between them. If they fail to integrate these roles into their own relationship, then the image of parenthood takes over their ability to relate as individuals. Once identities become submerged in this way, the seeds of divorce may be planted. The ways in which women in particular become trapped in this pattern have been well-documented, in particular by Betty Friedan in *The Feminine Mystique*, but some men also can be pulled in two, at equal cost. One husband said: "Once our child was born I put all my energy into being 'the good father' and doing 'all the right things' until, in the end, the close relationship between Liz and I disappeared."

With basically no preparation for marriage, the pressures of having babies and bringing up young children can result in personality changes which render a couple divorce-prone. The amount of work needed to run a home and family, which falls mostly on women, can be exhausting. As the sociologist Ann Oakley points out: "Women just have too much to do; fifty hours of housework a week, child-care twenty-four hours a day plus meeting the demands of a husband."* To add to this many women are also doing jobs outside the home. These heavy demands in marriage are usually a stronger burden than can be anticipated and very difficult to deal with once they are there.

Men come under heavy pressure too. They very often have to live in two worlds—their daily work and family life in the home they come back to each day. Some have work which forces them to be away from home. If a man is made unemployed this puts strains on the marriage. Most men don't identify as strongly with the home as women—even women who have jobs outside the home—yet they are still usually providing the family's major income. This, combined with a sense of being neglected by their wives compared with the wives' attitude to

* *The Observer*, January 20, 1980

them before the children came along, can lead to feelings of being wanted only as a provider.

Men have the characteristic of being able to be very single-minded to the point where they can exclude other things going on which they ought to be attending to. This is how men achieve results in what they do whether at work or in a hobby. But this is hard for a woman to accept since she is forced by necessity to divide her capacity for singlemindedness among conflicting priorities. Though a man will concentrate for hours on his woodwork while the children get up to mischief and the dustbins have not been put out, a woman will be concentrating on several things at once—perhaps studying for an exam while keeping an eye on the cooking and listening out for the children. Her ability to do these things at the same time leads to resentment that her husband simply concentrates on one thing and ignores everything else. Behind this is a fundamental difference in approach to life between the majority of men and women.

In a family in particular a woman with a strong, feeling nature does most of the caring. She may complain about her husband's lack of feelings yet have missed the opportunity that the relationship provides to teach him about this area of life and show how he might express it for himself. Of course, this pattern has very deep roots going back to childhood upbringing and beyond. This is now an area which is rightly the concern of many feminists, but feminism has also shown that single-mindedness is necessary for women as well as men.

More hidden are the ambivalent feelings that many men have about being fathers. No longer being given the same attention they received before, they often come to feel that marriage is more a series of demands than a state of love and companionship. To take Ann Oakley's point, the total amount of work and pressures for both husband and wife created by having children is, for many, an almost impossible burden. Add to this the financial pressures that many families face, especially those on low incomes, and it is no wonder that many marriages crumble. Yet some families, somehow, cope with seemingly overwhelming difficulties which cannot break the bonds that hold them together.

In almost every marriage the partners are expected to involve themselves with each other's relatives. The benefits can be enormous but, equally, in some families demands and personality differences intrude into a relationship so severely that they may undermine it. For example, constant interference from a parent or parents of one of the partners can leave the couple no space in which to create a life of their own—which leads to resentment. Lucy told us: "For years Les and I more or less *had* to take holidays in his father's seaside bungalow in Devon. His father was a very forceful person and Les always felt obliged to go—and I went along with this until I could stand it no more. It was one of the reasons why we split up."

Having a child is one way in which some couples consciously try to save their relationship in the mistaken belief that this will draw them together. It may be their first child or a further child after they have had a family. The likelihood is that to have a baby in these circumstances will not make the underlying problems go away, indeed it can make things worse and even precipitate breakdown. In any case a child can rarely provide the glue to hold together a drifting relationship.

A cooling of the normal and established sexual relationship is an obvious sign of a troubled marriage. Fatigue and depression can run even a healthy sexual relationship into difficulties but where a couple's sex life simply declines to a low level it is likely to be linked to other things. For example, unresolved sexual and communication problems may have become a part of the marriage. A marriage which falls into set habits, including sexual ones, can become boring and disillusion will set in. We tend to expect, for example, that sex will stay at the same intensity and are disappointed if it doesn't happen this way. Equally, we have various demands about sex which may not be realised as the relationship develops. Sex, at its best, is an intensely personal experience. In the context of marriage pressures it may be very difficult for two people to accept and go along with the unique sex life each relationship creates. If we cannot adapt and explore the subtleties which occur we may feel incomplete. More starkly, these differences, if unresolved, could amount to incompatibility. This may also occur when a partner becomes aware of their need for sexual relationships with their own sex, a tendency they may have been aware of before they married.

A regular sexual relationship with one partner touches deep aspects of our personality. Success and difficulties in this area go back to childhood and adolescence, and the development of identity and self-esteem. Problems of communication in the relationship may be at their most acute when reflected in sex. A good example is "having to perform" where one person falls into a pattern of acting in a way their partner expects, or believes they expect, or where two people's needs from sex are very different. Like marriage itself, a healthy sexual relationship depends on a commitment which is continually renewed.

Having children often affects a marriage so profoundly that a couple's sexual life may never be the same again. The changes and pressures once they start a family may prevent them from resuming their normal sexual relationship. But, as we said earlier, these problems, like post-natal depression, can indicate serious unresolved differences between them.

Finally, sexual cooling may be reflected in one partner taking a lover. That person may be reacting to a feeling of rejection by and/or distance from their partner. Or they may look outside marriage for more stimulating company as well as better sex. The other partner may collude with this or not, or may be unaware of the situation, but either way the emotional gap which has appeared stands a good chance of widening to a gulf where the only solution is likely to be divorce. More than a third of Britain's divorces are granted on grounds of adultery.

When a relationship is breaking down, for whatever reason, changes are taking place; and the knowledge that change is occurring is the essential first step to working with it. It may be months, or even years, before one or both partners becomes aware of what is really happening because habits of everyday life act as a mask. When this realisation happens it may trigger feelings of insecurity—emotional or financial—sadness, anger, rage and a whole range of unfamiliar emotions. A feeling of "it can't be happening to me" is common, mixed with a heavy sense of inevitability which at first is usually pushed away. But it is important now to accept the reality of what is happening. This marks a further change in the atmosphere and the partner who knows may become visibly upset. They may become sullen or burst into tears yet deny, when questioned, that anything is wrong. It is at this point you must admit the problem and talk about it. This first step to talking takes courage. It may be the hardest thing to do because it is so painful to admit, even to yourself, and it is hard to know how your partner will react. Knowing that it will be painful to raise the subject and equally painful for your partner to hear, you may keep things to yourself for some time then find yourself confiding initially in a friend or relative.

Bill said: "I held my feelings in for so long that, finally, they burst out one day while I was talking to my sister-in-law. She seemed to know and was surprisingly sympathetic."

In Jackie's case her mother asked her point blank if she still loved Alan. "I told her I didn't and that was the first time that I admitted the situation to anyone else."

It is essential, now that the subject is exposed, that you do tell your partner your feelings. This is because you must accept the responsibility of dealing with the situation and also because you would simply be loading a third person with the burden of the secret. You can postpone the pain by not talking to your partner now but this leaves a burden with the person you have told.

The release of tension when the subject is brought into the open, with all its upsets and difficulties, makes a starting point. It is an opportunity for both partners to accept what is happening and begin to explore ways of coping. The mixed feelings involved, particularly failure and guilt, are hard to deal with—even frightening. It is hard to be rational and it may be some time before you and your partner can talk together constructively, if at all. What is now occurring is unique to each couple: a course of events with its own momentum which may last for a long time. Marriage breakdown has its own energy and is a process which has to be worked with.

The admission and acceptance we have talked about are a crucial stage in reaching the right state of mind to have some control over what follows in the months ahead. It is here, we believe, that the foundations for an amicable divorce, if the marriage has to end, are laid. Yet the commitment this demands is not an easy one. It involves facing and dealing with anger and hurt in yourself and in your partner and considering whether separation and divorce might be necessary. It involves talking about what changes you plan to make, what is best for the children and, where necessary, talking through issues which should not be left in the air.

A dialogue about these things is not always possible but not dealing with them has a lasting influence on people long after the divorce papers are through. To deal with the issues and not shirk them is painful and in the short term an option which seems unnecessary, even masochistic. Why talk about these things when it must surely be better to get the whole business over with as quickly as possible? Our answer is this: that the pain is a necessary healing process which will help you resolve doubts about yourself and guilt about the break-up, and which will channel deep anger into necessary outlets. In the longer term, you may regret that you did not try to deal with these factors now, and some of them could emerge as problems in future relationships.

It takes time to develop a positive approach but to recognise this as the goal at this stage affects the course of your future life. The support and dependence on which you have relied in marriage has to alter, leaving you to re-establish or establish for the first time a sense of true independence. You will need this independence to establish a new lifestyle within the relationship as it now is, and then possibly outside it later. This is partly because there will be an adjustment in the balance of emotional dependence between any two partners, and partly because habits, and ways in which they spend their time, will also undergo a change. This is a time to find inner strength to help you discover what you will want in life in the future. It is very much a test of your identity—a situation that demands that you examine who or what you really are or want to be.

To make these statements while still living with your partner can require considerable patience and skill; the situation may be tense, explosive or apathetic. The important thing is to work to dissolve communication blocks so that they do not become permanent. Sometimes it takes space, even separation, before two people can talk about their differences. Commonly all that happens is that the husband leaves and the wife has to cope with the children alone. Once two people are living apart it is even harder to give the time to talk which is needed—a lot may depend on what can be resolved while you are still together. Longstanding disagreements may come to a head at this time or arguments arise out of the situation. The way that you tackle these differences is a key to your relationship in the future—whether you stay together or not.

An unhappy marriage exposes underlying factors in both partners' emotional make-up. This is why the experience of breakdown is such a harrowing one. Arguments in this context are an expression of undeveloped areas of the personality, so that breakdown is one of the life crises during which a person is confronted with this (often irrational) side of their nature. The situation offers the opportunity to acknowledge that by altering your attitude you can deal more effectively with the immediate problems.

There are two kinds of arguments: constructive ones and destructive ones. We aim to show here how destructive tactics or slanging matches simply wreck the chances of reaching any progressive agreement. It is here that communication can stop permanently, leading to the familiar and expensive trail of bitter disputes, long talks with solicitors, court battles, fights over children and money—and resulting in the lifetime silence of the partner who refuses any further contact. This is the stuff of marital disputes which fills the columns of the popular press week after week, and most of it is avoidable. On the other hand, constructive ways of dealing with disputes and putting your point of view will minimise these upsets, establish understanding and enable you to solve the inevitable problems of marriage break-up.

The biggest single obstacle to getting anywhere in arguments is *not listening*. Continual arguments that get no further than the superficial issues masking the real ones, or repeated exchanges of insults, produce a stalemate because feelings get in the way. Many people are simply unaware of the strength of their underlying feelings when they argue and it is essential to get in touch with these feelings before anything can change. Often this pattern of response has originated in childhood and now colours their reactions as adults to any kind of dispute. Often disputes literally trigger sensitive areas which release feelings of insecurity, fear and anger which are otherwise dormant and this is why some people are impossible to deal with. They cannot move forward beyond the shouting match to begin to argue constructively.

However, it is important to realise that any argument is an *interaction* between two people. They may have fallen out over a particular issue: an affair may be uncovered, or they may start an open discussion of their differences. Couples who continually argue or bicker are locked in a pattern both sides are perpetuating, even if one partner makes most of the noise. It is important to listen actively now to what the other person is really saying. Arguments may be confused and slide off the point and go round in circles.

Often the real subject of the argument may not be raised, but somewhere within the dispute is the true issue. If you cannot find this issue and begin to deal with it then the help of a third party may enable a way forward to be found. Many people find a friend to confide in whose opinions they trust. Often such a person can provide some insights which may not have been considered before. But do not expect too much since a person who takes your side and merely backs up your opinions is not being really helpful. The friend who can listen without taking sides comes closer to the help you need, and may enable you to see the situation in a new perspective. These people are fairly rare but anyone who is helped in this way is very fortunate. For example, Roger, who moved into Jim's flat after an explosive row with Miriam, said: "I was very lucky. Jim was incredibly patient while I poured out my troubles. Though he did no more than listen, it helped me find the patience to go back and start to talk things through."

Some people spend their whole lives reacting to even trivial difficulties in an argumentative manner—in and outside marriage. Some argue only with their partners and show only their "good side" to the outside world, and again this is a pattern between partners. If you are married to someone who is like this, you are dealing with a non-listener par excellence, someone who cannot hear what the other person is saying because they usually get too wound up to separate the issues from their own internal anger. If your partner is like this in marriage, a break-up is usually stormy, traumatic and needs special handling to break the pattern because this kind of person feeds on continuing argument.

Take note if you are inclined to be like this yourself. The first rule is to try progressively to avoid getting drawn into more arguments. By not shouting back or making pointed comments you stop fuelling the urge in yourself to argue. The aim is to talk firmly and calmly, making essential points while knowing the direction you want the discussion to follow. If you feel you are getting no further, it is sensible to close the subject until another time. You can say, for example: "I can't talk any more about this now," or, "I need a break, let's discuss it tomorrow." It takes courage and persistence to adopt this approach together with time, considerable patience and acceptance of your own part in the problem. It may be months before there are noticeable changes but by sticking to it you take charge of the situation and gain some control over it, as we have said before. By refusing to provide the feedback that fuels the arguments, the climate can change, and the pattern will alter. In the calmer atmosphere that follows you can talk rationally for at least part of the time and find common ground.

A major difficulty when two people are in disagreement can be their different ways of seeing and dealing with problems. This stems from our individual psychological make-up. Men's strengths are often the logical rational functions of the mind— the capacities to calculate, invent, build and look at things from an objective point of view which are governed by the left hemisphere of the brain. On the other hand women's strengths are often the feeling, intuitive functions of the mind—empathy, artistic senses and non-logical thought processes governed by the brain's right hemisphere. These are different ways of knowing and of expressing ourselves which are balanced to a different degree in each individual and both are equally valid.

Where a person is dominated by one of these functions with the other undeveloped—as occurs in either sex—they may find it difficult to cope in situations where the undeveloped function should come into play. This can often be seen where a couple argues constantly without ever reaching any solutions. Each person is effectively talking a different language. More fortunate are those people whose rational and intuitive sides are equally developed for they can understand and relate more fully to a partner, and so deal with disagreements in a balanced way. Two people who function in this way can solve their differences far more constructively than those who cannot begin to understand each other's point of view. Communication can break down as a result of not recognising the other areas of the argument. It can also be seen in situations where a couple will not discuss their problems, and continue as if nothing is happening. Or it may be that one person realises that something is wrong but cannot get a response from their partner who refuses to acknowledge that there are difficulties. This very situation often produces the classic outcome where one partner suddenly leaves a marriage "without any warning" and the person left behind is totally mystified, having never realised anything was wrong.

Other barriers to effective communication are sarcasm, stubbornness and pride. Sarcastic comments are never helpful but merely express buried anger that twists the knife in any argument. More than this, sarcasm undermines the chances of reaching agreement or even the trust which must be the basis of any agreement. Similarly, persistent stubbornness shows a lack of willingness to meet the other person half way, and this is often at the root of those marriage break-ups which remain stuck in inflexible attitudes and lead to miserable and drawn out divorces. The positive side of stubbornness is that you may need to stick to your principles on some particular issue such as the welfare of the children, but beware if you continue to hold a fixed attitude on every issue. Stubbornness is strongly linked to excessive pride, where deep down a person feels that their identity is threatened if they concede anything in dispute to the other person. It is worth remembering that in a marriage argument, as in any other, the person you argue with is usually right some of the time.

Not everyone has the communication skills which enable the normal problems in marriage to be solved. These include being sensitive to others' feelings and realising the effect that words have on other people. Family patterns of upbringing have an important bearing on this. Families in which, for example, little opportunity for discussion is created, or where it is normal to say hurtful things to each other, do not foster the art of saying what you mean in a constructive way. In contrast, the skills needed to communicate properly are deliberately taught in the fields of industrial relations and business management, where the havoc that is caused by the lack of them is well recognised.

Some people instinctively have these abilities and it comes naturally to them to use a very definite technique when talking to others. For example, they will wait for a response after making a point in an argument which allows the other person to take in what has been said and make a reply. This may also show that the listener did not understand the point that was made and it might have to be clarified or explained in a different way. You can act similarly by listening and responding carefully. If you are receiving mainly abuse, it is usually better to ignore it and keep to the issue at hand or end the conversation until a better time.

The constructive use of silence during a discussion of differences provides two things. If you wait before replying after something is said, it shows the other person that you are prepared to listen to their view. It also lowers the temperature because you are less likely to blurt out unconsidered remarks which inflame the situation.

A second way is to try to be non-judgmental. This involves not rejecting out of hand what your partner may say. To disagree constantly will put them on the defensive and make them angry. To continue in this way arouses recriminations, blocks progress and suppresses the real issues. The aim is for each to allow the other person to say what they feel and move on progressively from there.

Finally, honesty is the thread which enables a discussion to move towards a conclusion, at least an interim one. Honesty means showing your true feelings so that your partner knows exactly how you feel. Honest anger is better than veiled insults and can clear the air even though this may be upsetting. Honesty also means that you should not hide any information from your partner that they ought to know. For example, if you have a lover you want to leave for, it is both unfair to hide it to avoid the repercussions and a mistaken kindness to believe you are sparing the other person's feelings by doing so. It is only then that the real issues can be openly discussed.

Constant arguments in the presence of children, or unresolved tension between their parents in the home, undermines children's emotional development and peace of mind. Parents and family are a very large part of a child's world and parents' unhappiness is often reflected in changes in their children's behaviour. These include temper tantrums, changed eating and sleeping patterns, difficulties at school and regression to an earlier phase of childhood. Serious and fundamental differences between adults should not be a part of the child's world— because children pick things up—and should be dealt with in privacy. In this way children are not pressured by the adult world they are too young to cope with.

Children's needs are often forgotten or ignored by parents who are too absorbed in their own problems. We talk more fully in a later chapter about how children can be helped when a marriage is in trouble, but it is worth mentioning here that once a couple begin to resolve the issues between them children's difficulties also begin to ease.

The psychologist Frances Wickes quotes a case of a disturbed girl aged about nine who was affected by her parents' cold relationship. They chose eventually to part and the girl's behaviour became normal again. As Frances Wickes says, she was "a victim of the wrong atmosphere in the home, and her trouble disappeared as soon as her parents settled theirs".*

* *The Inner World of Childhood*, Frances G. Wickes (Coventure)

Illness as a symptom of an unhappy marriage can be found in both adults and children. In adults this is expressed in many forms, some obvious and some more subtle, so that the person affected may make no connection between events in their life and what is happening to their body or mind. The widespread dependence of many thousands of women in Britain on tranquillisers and anti-depressants (psychotropic drugs) as they look after their husbands and families is a case in point. They are prescribed by doctors because of women's difficulty in coping with the special pressures in their everyday lives. Many of these women are seriously burdened, as Ann Oakley says, "with too much to do plus the demands of a husband", yet many others do not have such burdens but live comfortable, well-ordered lives in expensive homes. Such women, too, are on tranquillisers in large numbers—"the Surrey disease" as one pharmacist has called it. So these problems are not specific to marriage itself but are reflections of inappropriate lifestyles.

What can be the cause of an illness which affects people from such different backgrounds in the same way and requires strong medication to cope with it? We find ourselves looking again through *The Feminine Mystique* and Betty Friedan's descriptions of "the problem with no name". She identifies the difficulty facing almost every wife in one succinct sentence: "It is easier to live through someone else than to become complete yourself." We agree with her that this need for identity cannot be ignored, and that the question she posed in the 1960s "Who am I?" is still fundamental to everyone and not just to women. We also believe that the failure of many women to ask that question and then take responsibility for their own lives exacts a heavy price in the form of illness and unhappy marriage.

An increasing number of doctors are sure that many physical and mental illnesses cannot be divided from the psyche. When a person is under stress in an unhappy marriage we believe that there is a whole spectrum of illnesses to which partners of either sex may fall victim. An American psychiatrist Wayne Dyer, in a book on personality problems, says: "There is a burgeoning amount of evidence to support the notion that people even choose things like tumours, influenza, arthritis, heart disease, 'accidents' and many other infirmities, including cancer, which have always been considered something that just happens to people."*

Certainly in Britain the increasing use of marriage guidance counsellors in doctors' surgeries has produced benefits which, says the Marriage Guidance Council, can be clearly demonstrated. The council says doctors are openly admitting that they lack counselling skills that would enable them to treat the whole patient and they report a significant reduction in the need to prescribe expensive psychotropic drugs.†

The list of illnesses which fall into the category—the psychosomatic diseases—is elastic and at the present time partly speculative. For example, migraine and many skin conditions are widely accepted as psychosomatic in origin but no one can be sure yet to what extent heart disease, kidney disease and cancer follow the same pattern. However, a growing number of doctors are certain that these diseases have their origins in difficult and stressful situations in life, of which a collapsing marriage is one. As we said in our first chapter, the body, mind and emotions need to work together in harmony if a person is to maintain good health. Sometimes it is only when these deep areas are explored that the link between them can be grasped. This self-exploration can bring benefits at a number of levels, as the experience of one person shows:

A successful businessman who was unhappy at home and who suffered from arthritis in his hands and migraine finally found his way to a psychologist. Over a period of time she showed him that he was feeding his mind through his work but was unable to share his feelings in his marriage. The results of this imbalance were reflected in his physical condition. However, when he learned to get in touch with his feelings and show his wife more affection, his migraines and arthritis also eased.

People are not generally aware of the range of outside help that is available for those in marriage difficulties. In particular, we are talking about counselling and psychotherapy, in which, either alone or with a partner, different ways of dealing with the problems may be found. This is usually done at meetings,

* *Your Erroneous Zones*, Wayne W. Dyer (Sphere)
† National Marriage Guidance Council Annual Report, 1982

normally lasting an hour, over varying periods of time.

Radio phone-in programmes which deal with listeners' personal problems are a form of counselling—a two-way conversation mixed with advice which begins to make each problem more manageable. We talk about the various kinds of help available in greater detail in the chapter on Professionals.

Many couples never think of taking this course, others flatly refuse to try it when the idea is suggested, and it is common to leave it so late to seek this kind of help that divorce is almost inevitable. Most people feel it is a brave step to talk to a stranger about their personal problems, but the insights and clarity which a trained professional offers can, with time and patience, shed completely new light on a difficult situation.

CHAPTER 4

The Meaning of Affairs

One way in which some people seek independence and a sense of identity is by having an affair or a series of affairs. This need was identified in the headline in a newspaper article on the subject which said: "Time and again people say an affair made them feel alive. It made them feel their lives were worthwhile."* Dissatisfactions and disappointments with marriage were shown to be the main reason why people chose to have affairs. But in a revealing paragraph a woman described how, when she was "desperate and weary of life she decided against adultery and took a university course instead" her husband behaved exactly as if she was having an affair. She lied to get money for books and then read them secretly in the lavatory.

This episode gives a clue to the complex underlying reasons behind affairs and, equally suggests that affairs have a more significant part to play in the development of the individuals who are married than is generally realised.

The sense of something missing in marriage is a common one which people deal with differently. Some ignore it and plod on, leading a life where sex and affection take a back seat as involvement with work and children takes over. Busy professional people who have no children can find, after a while, their individual activities are more absorbing than sharing life with someone else. But then, as the divorce lawyer Blanche Lucas says, people expect too much from marriage anyway. Talking about the number of people who divorce in Britain she comments: "The fantasies they have about marriage lead one to suspect that there has been something unrealistic about their upbringing; they think they are going to live happily ever after; they expect complete rapport at every level; a perfect sex life—whatever that may be."†

It is no wonder, given the variety of reasons why marriage

* *The Guardian*, November 22, 1982
† *The Observer*, February 28, 1982

can pall, that people seek sexual companionship elsewhere. The
search for romance and excitement is universal and in people
who are truly alive lasts throughout life. The lives of many are
made interesting by the exhilaration of a challenging job, an
engrossing sport, by other highly creative leisure activities in
the arts, or by travel. Having an affair can fulfil a similar need
but it can also fulfil deeper ones relating to every person's need
for affection, for being valued and for being accepted for
oneself. More important, these qualities confirm our individual
identity at the most intimate levels and lack of them, especially
in marriage, amounts to deprivation. It is the intimacy of
marriage and other close relationships which provides this
exchange but one which most individuals expect to include a
number of different qualities—the emotional links of close
sexual relationships. These links are suggested in the diagram:

Lover

Friend △ Companion

When we marry we marry a lover, we also need a true friend
and the nurturing and acceptance that companionship brings.
When all these qualities are functioning together the relationship
takes on a spiritual quality in the broadest sense. Often, though,
they are not all there in the first place or else become lost or
submerged as marriage slips into routine. To seek a lover is to
admit (even if unconsciously) one or more of these elements is
missing in the marriage, and to look for them in another person.
Some people do achieve a balance of what they want by finding
it in two or more relationships but more usually a person will
try to find in a lover all that they wanted from marriage but lost,
or perhaps never had. At their most acute these feelings are
behind the action of lovers who dramatically run off together,
yet this illusion is putting the same unrealistically high demands
on the new relationship as on the old one. This is why so many
affairs run their wayward course only to end in unhappiness.

The risks and furtiveness which affairs involve reveal another
underlying reason why people embark on them. Enjoyment of
the secrecy and intrigue that is involved seems to provide its

own raison d'etre in many cases. The thrill of meeting and having sex with someone unknown to your partner, and perhaps to theirs too, provides a level of excitement which may not be present in a person's everyday life. There are people who, by nature, need to test themselves and take risks throughout their lives and to whom an affair is a part of expressing this urge. But persistent affairs suggest a continuing adolescence and behaviour which is unconscious even to the extent that a person never takes real risks of any sort in their everyday life. By refusing to grow up they are diverting creative energy which could be used more productively.

In her book *Putting it all Together*, the American psychologist Irene Kassorla relates extra-marital affairs to the notions taught during childhood that sex is dirty. The result, she says, is adults who seek illicit sex because they cannot enjoy open sex with their partners.

"Extra-marital sex can keep the man a little boy or the woman a little girl. Lying, stealing, cheating, hiding from Mommy or Daddy is what little boys and girls do. People who are cheating on their mates are duplicating these childhood behaviours. The married man or woman who is promiscuous may still be hanging on to early childhood behaviour."*

Dr Kassorla says affairs can also be understood as a prime vehicle for anger and "used as a substitute for anger when one partner is furious and can't express the anger directly". Instead of standing up to the partner over some issue, someone will get their own back by having sex with someone else. It is worth quoting what she says next:

"But the affair is like a smokescreen. It creates distance and keeps you from seeing what is really happening within your marriage. You're so happy with your lover that you become blind to *your* role in the pain of your marriage. It prevents you from looking at *your* part in the problem."

This brings us to the idea of taking responsibility. Since affairs are normally an outward sign of marriages in trouble, there is an obligation sooner or later to look at the whole situation you find yourself in rather than be carried along by it.

* *Putting it all Together*, Irene Kassorla (Warner Books 1973)

It is a question of taking control of your life and working through the problem areas. When we fail to do this our family life, work and our whole lifestyle may crumble. A partner in a busy architect's practice and one of the secretaries fell passionately in love and they began spending long lunch hours together. After a few weeks they were spending every available minute in each other's company and their work suffered to the extent of hardly being done at all. For some time their colleagues filled a lot of the gaps but eventually they became angry at the heavy work load. Finally the other partners could no longer overlook their colleague's inability to do his job and he was forced to take a less responsible job in another part of the building. Soon afterwards the affair petered into stalemate, his career lay shattered and he was left with the long haul to put the pieces back together at home.

Women frequently find themselves trapped in the position of falling in love with men who are not really free and some repeat the pattern again and again. In America an association, Other Woman's Forum, has been formed to counsel women having affairs with married men. The main problem is the inevitable unhappiness which stems from falling in love with a man who usually remains securely married. As one woman puts it: "When he fails to get in touch for days or weeks—as he will when there is pressure of work or a risk of detection—then I sit in abject misery, getting bitter, feeling vindictive about the casual treatment I am getting; but there is no one to vent those feelings on." This tortured waiting for the phone to ring is a picture of a typical *teenager* in love.

Surprisingly, the Forum's object is to strengthen the position of "The Other Woman" by telling her that she cannot help falling in love and that she need feel no guilt. When you examine the selfishness and helplessness that is being justified by this approach, it can be seen that women who find themselves in this situation are being encouraged to remain passive and to take no responsibility for their lives, or to consider others. Take this quote from one of the other women:

"The Other Woman is not an ogre, she is just a woman who loves a man so much that she is willing to take what little she can get, live on the fringes of his life, and if that isn't true love, what is?"*

But love isn't about being a doormat. To behave in this unbalanced way is to have very little self-esteem. It raises questions of lack of identity and inability to create a happy life for oneself—even an unconscious urge to seek unhappiness. True love involves two people who care for and respect the person they love whether they live with them or not. The caring and respect in this particular common situation are, sadly, all one way.

There is a strong element of self-labelling and labelling by society in the terms "other woman" and "mistress" which seems to encourage, or even create, a particular kind of stereotyped behaviour.

Polly Toynbee in a *Guardian* article about mistresses says: "After talking to all these women I was left with the bizarre impression that they had all been talking about the same man. He was gentle and affectionate but hopelessly weak and indecisive ... what's more, all these men apparently had the same wife. She was cold, distant, only wanted marriage for the social status and the children. She was middle-aged and had never lived alone, or worked... It turns each of them into crude caricatures, losing their individuality and their dignity, playing out this bad melodrama."†

The promptings of the unconscious can lead us into all kinds of situations. As we showed in the opening chapters, a person can have several sides to their nature with different energies that need expression. Those with a dual nature may be content with the person they married yet have affairs to satisfy an adventurous streak. However, this may have less to do with love than an inner drive that is attempting to integrate these two parts of their nature.

At a practical level there are attitudes and responsibilities to be looked at. If this is what, as an adult, you feel you need, has this need been made clear to your partner and their feelings taken into account? Are you prepared to allow them the same freedom

* Reported in *The Daily Mail* December, 1982
† *The Guardian*, October 31, 1983

if they need it? Marriage creates bonds at an emotional level which women generally take more seriously than men. To many men a "one night stand" is of little importance emotionally yet, if discovered, it can completely undermine a wife's trust. An affair can sometimes be dismissed in the same way. Men tend to underestimate the deep feelings and commitment that the majority of women bring to marriage. Even fleeting sexual relationships are rarely as casual for a woman as they seem, because her feelings are usually so much stronger than a man's. In a brief relationship or in marriage it is often the woman who is supplying most of the feelings. This is why it is so much easier for many men to walk out of a relationship, including marriage. Their desires may have been aroused but their feelings—the unconscious feminine side of their nature—will still be relatively dormant and therefore uncommitted.

Men have their feelings too, but find it difficult to talk about them with their men friends. In any case, for men to share their feelings with other men is generally discouraged in Western society. While women can usually spread parts of their emotional life among their women friends, a married man is expected to channel most if not all of his through his wife. This social pressure can only be an incentive to start an affair.

An affair may be the first outward sign of an inward urge towards change in both men and women. Where the role, conventions and practical demands have taken over an excessive part of the whole, the psyche may rebel and, through external events, force a person to take note of the parts of their personality which are being neglected. Traditional marriage with its life-long commitment to one person is a very constraining institution when looked at in the light of the many variations in human nature. Until this century it appeared to work, though this may be more a function of social pressures and the fact that life expectancy was shorter. Society generally insisted on life-long marriage; roles were more clearly laid down and, of necessity, the majority of people were concerned with the means of survival, not the luxury of personal freedom or self-development.

For many people a lifetime of conventional monogamous

marriage is ill-suited to the psyche's need for continuing change, and change usually occurs whether or not we consciously seek it. When a person finds they have altered and their husband or wife is no longer a person they can relate to, or even blocks their individuality, life becomes complicated. These situations create deep dilemmas which go beyond society's moral attitudes. They may be very hard to resolve and cause great pain and difficulties however a person acts. There are no set solutions and it is for each person to act with responsibility and, as far as possible, in a caring way to minimise the pain. In our culture divorce tends to be the main way that we can deal with affairs but this sometimes raises as many problems as it appears to solve.

It is when we take a look at attitudes to sex and marriage in other cultures that we can see how we create some of these stresses by our own deeply held beliefs about what marriage must be. Marriage and fidelity can be interpreted in different ways. The unrealistic demands that Blanche Lucas describes look very different when set beside the views held by other societies. Perhaps we can explain by looking at just one very different culture. Duncan Pryde, in a book about his life with the Eskimos of northern Canada in the 1960s, writes: "Eskimos don't think of sex in the romantic way we do. An Eskimo woman doesn't fall head over heels in love as we would say. Marriage is a practical matter to her, and sex is something else again."*

Pryde describes the Eskimos' openness about extra-marital sex in some detail, showing how anger, jealousy and guilt, so common in the West, are of much less importance in a society with a different moral code.

"There was no question of adultery or any feeling of shame... As long as a man or woman chooses someone outside his or her kinship circle, any arrangement agreeable to the persons concerned was possible."

He found that though some Eskimo men and women were promiscuous, most of these relationships were exchanges between husbands and wives, the product of comradeship in a

* *Nunaga*, Duncan Pryde (Corgi)

hostile land. Various conventions had to be observed but the main rule was to ask first.

'Normally, a man would never ask for an exchange relationship unless he were virtually certain the woman's husband would agree. Nor would he risk an illicit arrangement unless he was prepared for a violent reaction.''

Pryde, a single man, found himself invited into a relationship by Niksaaktuq, the eager young wife of Nasarlulik, a hunting companion and close friend, with Nasarlulik's full agreement.

"Do you desire my wife? Well, Niksaaktuq likes you and I like you too, so if you want to get my wife (and that was the term he used) then go ahead.''

Where two men shared a wife in this way, Pryde says, the men's relationship deepened and each also took on responsibility for the welfare of the other and his dependents should he fall ill. Although this approach to sexual relations developed as part of one society's means of surviving in a harsh climate, it shows that our own, more comfortable society, may have something to learn about dealing with a married couple's individual emotional needs and the sexual feelings which exist independently of marriage.

One way in which part of our society tries to allow expression of these needs is husband and wife swapping and "key" parties—the phenomenon of some modern housing estates. But what appear to be flexible relationships that enable people who are married to experiment sexually with others, often have flaws which make the practice often unsatisfactory or even destructive. Unlike the Eskimos, couples who freely offer their partners after cocktails lack the wider bonds and take big emotional risks. Because key parties involve the emotions of everyone concerned being set aside, they hold the dangers that one person may fall in love, another may be an unwilling participant, or the shallow feelings which the "roles" demand may expose and hazard a couple's marriage. The outcome may be the opposite of what they intended.

Affairs so often create havoc and unhappiness and act as a prelude to divorce that the more positive changes an affair can produce are rarely noticed. Moral and social values create a climate in which the betrayal and transgression involved overshadow the affair's function in a wider sense. We fail to acknowledge, as the Eskimos have done, that a person, though married, may still need to develop through intimate—and not always sexual—relationships with others.

People need to achieve intimacy throughout life, and with both sexes, but it very often happens that an intimate relationship with someone of the opposite sex naturally progresses into a sexual one. A sexual relationship often initiates a learning process whether we want this or not. And so one sexual relationship in adult life may be insufficient to meet our needs at this level of learning—where our unconscious is prompting us. The psyche's urge to become whole so that we use our capacities more completely is not easily denied and falling in love in "forbidden" circumstances becomes a test of our deeper convictions. The responsibility that Duncan Pryde talks about is an important factor in any affair. To balance personal needs against commitments and responsibilities creates deep dilemmas because the need for relationship is so strong. It is the premium that we place on the sexual act which obscures this issue so that divorce tends to be the automatic "solution". Or is it?

When to tell your partner that you are having an affair is another dilemma. An affair so often follows a build up of difficulties in a marriage, of which either one or both partners may be aware. The person having the affair very often knows that there are problems in the marriage and even knows what they are. If they tell their partner, in a sense it is another way of bringing up their differences, a subject that needed to be raised earlier. This at last gives an opportunity to deal with the problems though it may be too late and too difficult by then to regain an emotional understanding. In this context the affair may be the tip of a very large iceberg, or a much smaller one when the couple can talk through the crisis and reach a new understanding. Cries of infidelity, which accompany many such revelations, may be hollow when set beside a long chapter of discord, upset or indifference which preceded the act itself.

Some couples are able to find a means of coping and working through the situation where one is having an affair. Jack became aware after some time that Tina was having a relationship with someone else. He was as much puzzled as hurt by what was happening but would not raise the subject directly. There was no row, no recriminations. Instead Jack elected to stand back and let Tina sort out what she wanted without any pressure from him. The affair finally ended, and although Jack did not want to face the reasons behind it stemming from the marriage, they reached a different understanding and stayed together.

In some cases open revelations may be the best thing that could happen despite the difficulties they raise. A marriage in which the person having the affair preserves the normal routine while suppressing feelings of discontent creates powerful undercurrents that may be sensed by the other partner and by children. The feeling of having to maintain a surface respectability but living a lie produces pressures which often manifest in acute guilt. Fear of the partner's response and the trouble that will ensue adds to this guilt which may become unendurable. A person may then lose the initiative of revealing the affair at a moment of their choosing so that instead the knowledge bursts out uncontrollably—though they may in effect allow themselves to be found out. Paul's experience shows one way in which this happens:

"I had a number of affairs over several years and even though this must have been obvious, Sue never seemed to notice. Our life of routine just continued. Then I started with someone who lived in the house exactly opposite. Inevitably Sue saw me leaving late one night and all my feelings came up into the open. I realised later I must have used this affair to force something to happen in the marriage. Now we are getting divorced."

We don't always have the courage to act responsibly when it is necessary. Consideration for the others involved in such complex areas of our lives is difficult to achieve, and the priorities are hard to define because we do not want to hurt other people. The need to give and receive at intimate levels with different people and how we cope with this is an area of emotional relationships that Western society is only beginning to accept.

CHAPTER 5

Talking and Making Decisions

Conflicting emotions surface when a marriage appears to near its end and this is a new and often frightening experience. A few people can distance themselves sufficiently and others can appear to. The feelings of confusion, guilt, anger, jealousy and perhaps fear which now erupt make it difficult to act calmly. Deep feelings of desperate loneliness can overtake and engulf everything. You may feel completely unable to cope with everyday living—you may burst out crying, feel physically ill, or your body may just ache all over. At work you may sit in a daze unable to concentrate, leisure activities may be undertaken listlessly or with aggressive concentration, and at home with the family the atmosphere can be strained and distant, or argumentative.

Once this situation is reached it is time to break the patterns of disagreement and seek a new understanding of the problem. Human nature being what it is, we hope the problem will go away or get better of its own accord. But there is no use in just wishing things were better. At this stage of an unhappy marriage leaving things any longer only makes them worse. The best route in an unhappy marriage is to face the crisis and start working through the real issues, which may be obvious or still hidden behind a facade. This may make it necessary for one person to take the initiative to resolve things.

We recognise that to try to break this deadlock can seem impossible. This very sensitive and complex area of human relations is one about which there are no easy answers. But you must ask yourself honestly whether you are simply going through a bad patch, or whether the time has come to face reality and accept that the marriage could be over. We know from personal experience the tremendous emotional and practical pressures that arise once a person wants to do something about the problems of a deeply unhappy marriage. The emotional reactions cannot be predicted and changes that come now are profound and possibly irrevocable. These can mark the start of a long period of intense personal struggle in which there may be all kinds of setbacks. You may wonder at times whether it is all worthwhile: yet it is possible to build up a sense of certainty and confidence that the situation can be changed for the better in the long run.

There are important reasons for taking progressive steps now to reach a conclusion. It is unnerving and unsettling to live in a strained atmosphere for long because it invades all your thoughts and actions; it affects your self-esteem and sense of security; and the well-being of children may be affected. To try to resolve the situation involves actively caring for yourself and dealing with your partner in the same practical way that you would try to overcome an awkward problem at work, or elsewhere in the family. To make a very mundane comparison, you would be very unlikely to allow your car to deteriorate without doing something about it. A marriage in trouble is rather more important than your car. It is important to remember that this approach to marriage problems is valid at all times of life. The difficulties of divorcing at sixty may well be much more than those at thirty or forty, but the need for fulfillment and happiness is similar and can be sought and found at any age.

It is tempting here to pretend that everything is not all that bad. People are often prepared to put up with ways of living and all kinds of behaviour that they would not expect a friend in the same situation to accept. The unwritten rules of marriage seem to allow actions well beyond acceptable limits, so that impossible situations, even including frequent violence, will continue for as long as people are prepared to put up with them. Yet while this is going on, anger and resentment build up underneath and the situation can worsen in at least two ways: any remaining chance that you could stay together will be lost; or so much anger may build up that the divorce can only be a bitter one. Here, physical separation from your partner, such as a weekend away, can provide a breathing space to allow these feelings to be faced.

In this chapter we aim to show how getting to grips with the issues is both necessary and beneficial—and how it is possible to escape the pattern of unhappy marriage. There are some very useful techniques for bringing the issues out into the open and talking constructively to resolve them once and for all so that you can get on with living your life. For those in the most extreme situations, such as marital violence, we suggest ways of achieving some resolution based on the same principles.

It is very hard to try to understand the conflicting emotions which well up, such as the exasperation, anger and resentment that so many of us cannot help feeling. Understandably, we are not very good at talking about a sensitive emotional issue to someone else because we have never been trained to do it. Our feelings tend to take us over so that even minor issues become exaggerated in our minds and the big ones frighten us. Somehow, as we showed when we discussed ways of arguing (in the chapter on unhappy marriage), we must find constructive ways to say what we have to say and not be satisfied until answers are reached. This has to be a gradual, step-by-step process; it cannot happen overnight. It may take many weeks or months to arrive at a solution. But the most important factor is the approach and attitude you adopt. There may be different ways of dealing with the situation but there is a particular approach which works. It involves adopting positive attitudes, which can be described as: constructive, flexible, non-accusative and geared to problem solving. As we showed earlier in the book, there are two kinds of arguments, constructive and destructive ones. Similarly there are constructive and destructive ways of solving the present problems.

It is easier to talk about this than to carry it out since we instinctively blame and hit back, usually refusing to take *our* share of the responsibility for the situation. We readily see where the other person is at fault—in other words we external-ise the problems which, really, come from within the *two* people involved. Therefore, whatever the other person's actions, nothing can ever be wholly the other person's fault. It is very painful to ask yourself what part you have played, but to get anywhere satisfactorily it is necessary to do so.

Affairs are one of the most difficult situations in marriage and often force a couple to look closely at their relationship and to face the possibility of divorce. However, as we showed in our chapter on affairs, they are not as simple as they seem and divorce is not necessarily a solution. Before divorce is even considered the upset and highly charged atmosphere needs to be allowed to settle. This gives time to establish how serious a threat the affair is to the marriage. Initially it may be regarded, by all involved, as simply giving in to temptation. Many affairs are conducted only at this level—the word itself throws up an instant image. You may have to decide where you stand on this particular issue and act accordingly. But there is more going on at another level whether it is realised or not; to try to understand the importance of a particular affair or affairs at the emotional level makes it easier to reach decisions.

Is the affair perhaps a "necessary" one which is giving a man or woman experiences they feel they have missed in their earlier years before marriage? It may be a passing phase no matter how intense the affair is, even for a partner who moves out to live with someone else. Many a dramatic relationship of this kind fizzles out in the reality of everyday living. Or is it part of a pattern, a restless streak in your partner's nature? If so, you are faced with a choice of accepting this behaviour and that marriage may not be a big commitment to them, or of refusing to accept it. Is it a much stronger relationship which your partner needs in addition to the marriage or instead of it? Or you may be in this situation yourself. It may be that one of you has reached a point in your emotional development where a different kind of relationship is important. One vital area is the question of each person's needs and whether they are being met. If, say, you feel you are being given no affection or find it difficult to give your partner affection, this must be raised. Thus it is the crucial area of needs which must be frankly discussed and not merely the event itself.

There is no one solution to these dilemmas, but there is always a point at which you have to make a decision and act on it. People react in many different ways so before you act in haste consider other people's experiences. For some their partner's first affair ends the marriage as far as they are concerned. Others will accept and some merely tolerate a series of affairs and achieve a different balance in their relationship. Much depends on a person's needs and their level of maturity. One wife accepted two separate affairs her husband had and continued the relationship. But when he announced for the third time that he was seeing someone else she decided categorically that enough was enough and started divorce proceedings. She asked him to move out and though this affair also ended she stuck to her decision and refused to have him back.

When passions are high or the situation intolerable, it is extremely difficult to take that one step back and try to clarify your needs. From here you may begin to work towards what you want. This takes time. To make a hasty decision, like walking out of the house or deciding, in anger, to divorce is only a short-term solution and one almost certain to inflame matters. To leave a relationship, then properly disengage from it, is a much more complex process. To work through this process makes it easier eventually to reach an agreement which allows both partners to resolve the situation with dignity and on reasonable terms. This is crucial where children are involved because the repercussions may last *their* lifetime as well as yours if they have to share the burden of your continuing animosity.

Talking to the other person can raise its own problems according to their temperament. Some people will deny that anything is wrong, others can only shout when any subject involving the feelings is raised. There are people who are always convinced they are right and some who act in a bullying and authoritarian way whenever anything is discussed; those to whom any criticism strikes at their pride and still others who, when things go wrong, are never there to face the consequences.

One of the commonest problems here is to know what to say to your partner and especially how to begin. Although strong feelings may colour your attitude, try to put together the different aspects of the situation to enable you to raise the issues at stake and put them in a measured way. To get a response you could state frankly: "I'm upset and worried about our relationship and that you won't discuss it with me. I may be assuming

84

things which are not the case such as . . . and I want to know. Could we please find time to talk about it?" This approach makes it less likely that you will merely complain about each other and go round in circles, never getting beyond the accusations. You could also say: "It's hard to say this, but I've realised for some time that things have changed between us. I am not happy and there is something I want to say. . ." This involves telling your partner what is on your mind and asking them what they are feeling or thinking. Try to agree together what the situation is as you both continue to talk.

People are complex with different sides to their natures and it helps to time your approach. A legacy of difficulties going back over several months or years cannot be resolved in one evening and there are right and wrong times to discuss them. Few people are in the right mood to talk immediately after a day's work in or outside the home. It is far better to wait until you have eaten a meal and rested before raising the subject. It is better to sit down, in chairs at the same level, and then begin your discussion. This immediately involves both partners in the discussion and allows them direct eye contact. To try to discuss important issues while doing some other task, or at bedtime when tired, defeats the object of achieving direct communication. But privacy is all-important. If there are children or relatives in the house, wait until they are in bed or choose a time when everyone is out. If necessary, make an "appointment" to talk at a specific time.

One of the most difficult responses to deal with is where a partner maintains a silence and will not discuss anything. There may be fear behind their unwillingness to confront the problems, or plain obstinacy. Because differences in temperament become exaggerated, a reliable friend could "interpret" how you are feeling and some progress may be made this way. If you feel able, some reassurance through a gentle approach may enable you to open a discussion about the change in the relationship. If this approach does not work, this leaves you with little alternative but to explain, perhaps in a written note, that you intend to take some initiative to improve matters. Making this move may produce a response but where it does not you have to act for your own well-being. One woman whose kind but uncomprehending husband refused to enter any conversation about the rift in their marriage said: "I wish now I had shouted at him to make him take notice because he would not see how unhappy I was." He was unable to see that her needs had changed and they later divorced.

The situation where a partner will not discuss anything, or denies that anything is wrong with the relationship, is one which many wives in particular have to face. The phlegmatic, dutiful husband who works hard to provide for the family may well see his role mainly as a provider and be more concerned with the protocols of family life than with the emotional undercurrents, which to him may be irrelevant. He may not even be aware of them. For these reasons his wife may be left to act out the emotional and feeling element of his life for him and so he underestimates her capacity to function as an independent person with needs of her own. This undercurrent can show itself in several ways as, for example, in his resentment if she returns to work after many years running a home.

In a marriage with set roles of this kind, a woman who is changing and wants to express herself more fully after years of being "the dependent wife" may find it very difficult to convince her husband what is happening to her. She has to struggle against the situation she finds herself in and against the inertia of her own role in the marriage. Since she may have left the decision-making parts of the marriage to her husband, her attempts to assert herself and make changes are very much a personal struggle. As her awareness of the rift grows she is likely to feel an inner inevitability, mixed with guilt and loneliness, that she has to stand on her own. This brings with it the realisation that a break up will involve the loss of status and the security she has enjoyed and which have been a major part of her identity up to now. She will have to find a new sense of identity within herself.

The partner who can only shout when any issue to do with the feelings is raised is also denying that anything must alter in the marriage. A man whose feelings are just beneath the surface may react very quickly indeed to anything he feels is disruptive.

To him the idea of a serious talk about marriage is likely to be seen as very threatening. Even where there is no clash, no arguments or little said, one or both partners may not want to delve into the real issues, or be unable to. Unless there is some kind of breakthrough, such as beginning to exchange feelings or accepting help, it becomes extremely difficult to repair the situation by finding common ground. Without this, any real relationship now simply dies although many couples who reach this point stay together and maintain the marriage.

Difficulties in marriage so strongly affect our sense of self-esteem and sense of status at such a fundamental level that they uncover the less pleasant sides of our character. European and Japanese societies in particular put so much emphasis on being "nice" and "polite" to others that the aggressive energy which is in all of us and often repressed may be powerfully released when a marriage goes wrong. A normally kindly person may become physically dangerous. Sadness, frustrations and depression may now surface so that the personality undergoes a complete change.

It is so easy to get caught up in disagreements that anger hides the opportunities to deal with them in a mature, adult way. It is easy to continue blaming the other person and directing your resentment at them. They may be doing the same to you and each of you may not even consider your part in the problem. But angry and difficult behaviour is really a part of all of us which, in these situations, takes us over. However, it is only a part of our personality and the other, more positive, sides are still there. When you are not getting on with somebody don't let the "bad" side of their nature cut you off from this "good" side. They are both part of the same person. To remember this creates the opportunity to relate to them on a level which leads to resolution.

How well you truly know your partner can make a crucial difference to how you get through to them. Everybody has a positive side to their nature which can respond when the right approach is made. One person will respond to an appeal to their sense of fairness, another to their compassion. A person with a competitive spirit might respond to a challenge to achieve a solution. This is all part of the skills of understanding and communication which you will have to develop at this time. To make yourself clear, express only what you are fed up with and what you want for yourself. The words you use are important since people tend to be taken over by their emotional reactions to what they hear. For this reason, words have to be chosen with care. Arguments are one thing but exchanging insults, or opinionated views, achieves the opposite effect since this involves using words which only inflame the situation.

All this involves trying to assess yourself and your own feelings and needs beyond the anger and frustration that is almost inevitably present. The skill with which you do this will decide to a great extent the way events progress towards a well-intentioned solution. It makes little difference whether you are angry or upset by what your partner may have done, or the other way round; it is still necessary to get beyond the anger in order to communicate. Where there is a lot of emotion present it is extremely hard to establish and accept the truth of the situation. Perhaps someone does not want to admit they are having an affair, or a partner may feel their behaviour is being questioned in some other way.

Arguments may be necessary to relieve true feelings and clear the air. However, people's ability to express their feelings varies widely. While some people will control them, others bottle them up so that they erupt under stress, making communication difficult, if not impossible. The build-up of unexpressed feelings and its release is behind many acts such as irrational outbursts, physical violence against a partner and child battering. With effort and some goodwill on both sides progress can be achieved in all but extreme circumstances. By applying some of the suggestions we have made and looking at methods of your own, better ways of communicating can be found.

One unhappy wife who finally left realised that for years there had been a pattern in which her husband coped easily with criticism but responded best to praise. She used this knowledge to improve the atmosphere between them by reducing her criticisms of him and giving praise where it was due.

To realise without warning that your partner considers the

marriage is over and is planning to leave can come only as a considerable shock, and a devastating one if your partner has suddenly left. The abrupt transformation of normal life into upset and uncertainty immediately makes an emotional mark which can last a long time.

The initial feelings of shock, bewilderment and disbelief can be considerable. There may be other feelings too: anger and a fierce sense of betrayal, particularly if your partner is involved with someone else. After the first blow it is very hard to even believe the reality of what is happening, or make any sense of it.

If you are the person who has been left by your partner, whether or not you were aware it was going to happen, your position is one of passivity. Your partner has made the active decision to go and you have not been given a choice. Though the early feelings of shock and bewilderment are more acute when a partner leaves without obvious warning, we believe that if this happens some changes in the relationship will have occurred. You might not have been aware of them or have picked up the signals. It could be that you realised that something was wrong in your relationship but did not talk about it or deal with it in any direct way. You may have dismissed this notion, feeling that the marriage was safe and "it could never happen to me". Feelings of anger and vulnerability you may now have are mixed with those of both blaming your partner and a sense of some responsibility for causing the breakdown.

Marriages are built on trust and this is strained to the limit when your partner wants to leave. It is important to try to preserve and even rebuild the trust element, which may break down completely unless you can see the real person through your emotional upset. Remember, your relationship has been trusting in the past and many areas of trust can remain if you allow it. The development of some trust from this point is crucial, because it will help to determine the possibility of reconciliation or the sensible handling of divorce. This is a period of great confusion, but remember that no one person is at fault, nor is one of you wholly to blame for what has happened—and time does heal. These words will not take away the pain and upset you may be feeling and you might need some help from a friend, counsellor, your minister or a doctor to help you to cope.

It takes courage to begin to accept what has happened to you and to recognise some of the patterns of the marriage which have led to the parting. You might have to accept that your partner does not want to come back and the truth will hurt. They may be leaving you for someone else after having considered it for some time. Yet there is a positive side when a relationship breaks down in this way, because gradually you *can* come to know yourself more completely and feel secure.

You may desperately want the marriage to continue, and any talking you are able to do will bring your views into the open and could give you a different perspective. Your partner may tell you that they feel something has been missing from the marriage. Whether or not you can accept this, it is important to try to express your own feelings. Depending on the kind of person he or she is, you may be given explicit reasons why they want to leave; or they may be unable, or not want, to communicate. They may not do so to spare your feelings or avoid an argument.

Your partner might simply feel an urgent need for a breathing space, after years of marriage, in which to find themselves and to consider their future. They may not have been able to tell you this as they might not have recognised it themselves. The urge to break out in this way sometimes comes unexpectedly. One woman in her forties who was comfortably married found herself saying, out of the blue, to a friend one day: "I am going to leave my husband." This was the first time she was aware of these feelings. Her women friends understood but her men friends found her intentions "unthinkable". A personal struggle now began as she came to realise that she had unused talents to explore and needed complete independence. She and her husband did divorce.

If you are considering leaving your partner, then try to consider first how you might feel or react if this happened to you. It is one of the most powerful ways you can reject someone and it can severely shake their self-confidence. You might feel

90

unable to tell your partner the truth and face the possible reactions but it could save a good deal of bitterness to give some warning of what you are planning—unless threats to your safety leave you with no alternative. There could be aspects of your marriage that you have not even considered and which you would benefit from knowing. To talk will probably release tensions which have been present in the relationship for a long time. By not doing this now it is difficult to avoid carrying an unconscious burden of unspoken thoughts which upset your emotional life and can lead to regret.

To leave suddenly denies your partner the opportunity to begin to work through feelings of rejection. These may exist on both sides—the person who leaves may have felt rejected during the marriage, while the person who is left faces rejection when the relationship breaks up.

Whatever the circumstances, the person you are leaving will be very hurt and find it difficult to believe what you say. It is now up to you to show ways in which you can still be trusted and be reliable over any arrangements that have to be made. For example, if you are supposed to pay maintainance, provide it as promised. If there is an arrangement for access to children, stick to it as far as possible so that the children are ready to be collected/returned, or that you collect and return them at the agreed time. Trust established at this practical level helps to reduce friction at an emotional level.

Occasionally there seems to be no alternative to leaving abruptly. For some people this may be the only way to break the bond of their relationship, which to them has become meaningless or destructive. By making this choice you are taking a course which has its own obvious difficulties; yet the practical and emotional adjustments needed still cannot be denied. After having achieved the physical and emotional distance you can set your mind to dealing with all the ensuing problems of separation.

If you are left behind and continue to love your partner, and cannot bear them going, you may hope as the months pass that they will come back. Occasionally this happens, but you will have to judge when to accept that there will be no reconciliation.

A gut feeling may tell you that the marriage is over but it is often better not to make any hard decision about this for some time since the situation remains an open one while emotions are worked through. Since you are forced into doing things independently, you can gain valuable confidence by putting this to use. Often separation gradually shades towards a more permanent state as daily habits begin to change. Meanwhile, use this opportunity to take a hard look at yourself, perhaps with outside help. There may be, for example, areas of your personality affecting the relationship which you were unable to develop in the marriage as it was and which can now begin to mature.

It can take months, even several years, for someone to come to terms with the reasons why their partner wants to leave. It is possible to accept that your partner wants something different in life. If you are the one who has decided to go, it may take patient talking to explain your feelings, but a point is reached eventually where explanations have to stop and the other person has to cope with their feelings. Do try to keep a bridge of communication open. This can be done through a friend or through the contact which is made in looking after children.

What we are suggesting may appear to be a completely new approach to dealing with problems. It may be that the openness of earlier years has been lost, so it requires time and persistence to re-establish this kind of exchange—or to learn it for the first time. The idea is to clarify the situation and this could involve going over a lot of ground about what led up to recent events. The initial reaction may be very emotional or deadpan, or your questions may be pushed aside and this can block your first attempts to open a discussion. But don't be put off talking since nothing can be resolved without being frank.

When a partner refuses to acknowledge that there is a problem and will not discuss it, then if this attitude persists you may have to consider forcing the issue in some way if anything is to change. You may have made some assumptions about the situation that are not entirely right, but nevertheless you cannot know where you stand without some feedback.

By now you may feel the need to discuss the situation with a third person. You should make it very clear to your partner that you are taking this step. For example, by exploring your own feelings with a counsellor or by talking to a solicitor, the situation may become clearer to you so that the next step becomes apparent. This will also show your partner that you are anxious that something should be done.

Although we talked at some length about arguments and ways of communicating in the chapter on unhappy marriage, we have felt strongly the need to enlarge upon this theme here. If we were asked to summarise this approach in a few words they would be: step back; establish what you want and *communicate*. These ground rules are worth supplementing with a few dos and don'ts:

Do express your feelings	Don't make constant
Do create a dialogue	accusations
Do be honest	Don't swap insults and put
Do stand up for yourself	downs
Do try to be flexible	Don't hide the real issues
Do remember that you	Don't be a door mat
were both happy once	Don't reject any positive ideas
	Don't forget that time *does* heal

Throughout this book we are offering a number of ideas and approaches to dealing with what are complex circumstances but, nevertheless, the scales are often loaded in different ways against both men and women. Many men find it extremely difficult, and some practically impossible, to express their feelings to their partners. Instead, their feelings may be held back by a mask of traditional behaviour which is difficult to penetrate. This, in part, is what drives many wives to the point where they seek care and affection elsewhere. Equally, for many women, it is still extremely difficult, and for some practically impossible, to assert themselves to say what they want, and to achieve individuality beyond the role their husband requires of them. This, paradoxically, drives many husbands eventually into relationships with women who give and take on a more equal basis. However, it may not always work out like this.

Sometimes what seems to be a totally new kind of relationship can turn out to have a similar pattern to the last.

Deep ingrained attitudes reinforced by society's stereotypes of marriage roles are often huge stumbling blocks to couples in a marriage crisis and may even provoke it. Lack of awareness of themselves beyond these roles and of the part that feelings and assertion play in everyday life creates misunderstandings for both sexes and prevents a true dialogue.

People find many reasons for not taking the steps to free themselves from a marriage they believe is empty. Their inner knowledge that the marriage has effectively ended is opposed by all kinds of thoughts and principles which make them hang on and be reluctant to leave. For example, strict beliefs that a marriage should never be dissolved may itself be a rigid attitude which traps them. Some people strongly resist any idea of leaving because any loss of status and standard of living is unthinkable to them. It *is* a huge decision to leave a marriage because it is the most complicated and distressing change we are likely to make in our lives. The ramifications can extend into almost every area of a couple's lives, forcing changes in personal relationships, family networks, work patterns, and bring domestic as well as emotional upheavals. Further, the values to which you may have held firmly may be turned upside down, so that you are forced to see life differently. It is at this point that you may decide to divorce.

There are many common fears and apprehensions which surface at this time and they can have such a paralysing effect that a person may stay in an empty marriage for years before they finally go, or never leave it. These feelings are powerful because often they relate to habits, views and attitudes which belong to us as individuals, to our sense of who we are. To deal with a marriage crisis you may have to say "no" or make a painful choice for the first time in your life. This may also involve adopting attitudes very different to some you held before.

The feelings which arise and are common to many are fears of the unknown, of being alone, not knowing where you will live or what the future outside marriage will hold, and the belief that

94

you will be no happier anywhere else. You may be afraid to face the disapproval of family and friends and worry about the children's future. You may also want to cling to the home and lifestyle you have become accustomed to over the years. These insecurities bind us to the situation we are in and test our ability to work through the problems and get our priorities right. If the marriage is intolerable it is helpful to understand that the doubts and insecurities we have may be blinding us to how things could change and improve outside the marriage. The fear of being alone does not mean that you will be alone—new friends soon appear in the life of someone who does their best to make a new start, even if some old ones are lost. The belief that you can be no happier anywhere else is not only being pessimistic but allowing your doubts to block your self-confidence. These doubts deny your capacity to create a happier life elsewhere. Leaving what you know and what is familiar is harder the older you become, but you may still have to do it.

The disappointment that family and friends are bound to feel when they learn of a couple's decision to break up can strongly inhibit some people from making any change. A person who is aware that most of their friends see them and their partner as "happily married"—perhaps the ideal couple—find it very hard to admit openly that the relationship is otherwise. Worries that a break-up will be met by disappointment and disapproval are very real, because the situation itself may touch off insecurities in others, even including colleagues at work. These feelings in others have to be acknowledged but nevertheless what is necessary for the individual, and the couple, needs to be worked through.

Apart from the natural upset, in some families the disapproval of relatives presents enormous pressures and obstacles to someone desperately trying to solve their marriage problems. The first mention of separation or divorce may be treated as a betrayal of shared values. However, the sense of guilt that can be engineered to keep "the family" intact at all costs is essentially a form of manipulation which denies a couple in difficulties the right to control their own destiny. This is a very different attitude from the genuine family concern in which parents and other relatives may offer help and understanding without interfering.

It can be deeply upsetting to contemplate the effect of a break-up on those close to us such as elderly parents, and how the lives of children might be changed with only one parent at home. We tend to forget, though, that children are naturally resilient despite the hardships and, with help and reassurance, better able to cope than we imagine. We talk further about children's responses and how they cope in the next chapter.

Marriage break-up can make us feel vulnerable and insecure in many ways of which one of the most alarming can be our worries about material status. Many of us become so attached and used to our home and lifestyle that we imagine our world falling apart for ever if these are threatened by the radical change that divorce brings—to the extent that this may be the major reason we cannot leave when all other indications say we must. Yet someone to whom a settled or particular lifestyle is important may be the person best motivated to establish these things quickly elsewhere—once they have made the break. One of their needs may be to become aware of this.

Concerns like these which make us hang on are often related to elements of our personality which we need to confront and work through to gain a better perspective and balance within ourselves. The break-up process itself exposes these very difficulties in our make-up and also produces the opportunities to do something about them. So there is a two-fold process here; one involves achieving as an individual the inner strength and security needed to start resolving particular emotional blocks and the other is using this approach to deal with the relationship problems of separation and divorce. They are so closely intertwined that they become as one. This is a challenge which not everyone realises exists and can accept, but it is primarily an opportunity which enables both partners to change and develop, though one may change more than the other.

It can be frightening to realise that it is necessary to come to grips with emotional situations which are completely new, but amidst the confusion this is a period of subtle change which, if recognised, can lead to new attitudes and greater self-confidence which will make the important changes easier. During this period a conflict with other feelings may make us resist change. For example, parents understandably find the effect of a break-up on their children difficult to cope with, even when they first consider it. It is felt keenly by both fathers and mothers although men often don't show it. The wives, and husbands, who stay in a marriage "for the sake of the children" are rightly concerned about their welfare because they love them, but when this becomes an over-riding concern it may deny other necessary areas of life which would enable a mother or father to achieve a balance and so lead a more satisfying life. The price, though, may have to be the break-up of the family and it may be a devastating choice to face. The many men who leave their families without apparent thought (and women too) may be denying the inevitable feelings of concern that are present, even if they are unaware of them. That these feelings exist is revealed partly in the problems which arise when a man who has walked out suddenly snatches the children, or takes an intense interest in them after a gap of months or even years without any contact.

A woman who always puts her family's needs first and ignores her own, or a man who always puts his own needs first and ignores those of his family have each to achieve a balance so that they value both themselves and others.

Similarly money, which may have produced problems for a long time, can be a very real and crucial obstacle to leaving. The loss of financial support and the hardship which may occur if a partner leaves, is itself sufficient to block expression of the underlying feelings which could help them deal with the prospect of break-up. However, our everyday lives and comforts can sometimes be an illusion in which our deeper disappointments and aspirations are put aside or repressed.

If you would far rather leave things as they are than have to cope with markedly reduced circumstances following break-up, consider why you are making this choice. It may be hard to judge which is the higher price to pay, whether to leave and be worse off financially or stay and suffer deep frustrations which eventually may become impossible to control. But many people who leave, or are left, find that they are a lot happier in spite of the hardships. In any case income and status fluctuate and financial security is far from guaranteed for anyone in today's difficult economic conditions. Incomes can go up as well as fall in changed circumstances. Despite the practicalities of little money there may be a lesson to learn here that involves attitudes about money's real importance. These attitudes can be revealed in many simple and apparently quite rational statements. For example, the man who, though his marriage is finished, says to his girlfriend he will not leave his wife because he cannot afford to is effectively saying he values his bank balance more than anything else. This is ironic considering that should his wife leave *him* he would have to face the financial difficulties anyway.

The conflicting feelings a person has to deal with at the point they decide to break-up can be shared with a friend, a relative or even someone they meet casually who has a sympathetic ear. Some people are naturally good counsellors. They are able to listen and often provide a way to see the problems more clearly. Though the listener may do nothing by way of giving advice they provide a sounding board which enables others to get in touch with their emotions. This is unlikely to provide any instant solutions but the act of expressing your feelings out loud helps to release them. Confiding in someone leads towards an understanding of the situation and helps to give a focus so that you can act.

You may be fortunate enough to know somebody who has the rare quality of being a good listener without making judgments when faced with someone else's problems. But be wary. People generally have built-in biases to their attitudes and are more likely to give unhelpful though well-meaning advice, or take sides, especially if they are close friends or relatives. Well-worn statements such as: "All men are the same", "Women can never be understood", or "If I were you. . ." have no value and only perpetuate disagreements. However, to confide in someone other than your partner at this stage, perhaps for the first time, may be the beginning of reflecting on your feelings and seeking professional help. Those who baulk at taking this step, but are fortunate to be able to talk with a supportive friend who has instinctive counselling abilities, may gain almost as much in working through some of the conflicts as if they had talked to a professional. At the same time, be prepared for the fact that the breakdown of a marriage often reveals views and attitudes which are obstacles to successful relationships and these may not change easily. The experience of the breakdown can give us insights into ourselves that we might never have expected.

A trial separation is one way to find the emotional and physical space many people need to come to terms with the difficulties of the past months or years. It is a big step to take but may be the one way to break free from repetitive patterns of disagreement and begin to see the realities of the situation and consider whether or not the relationship is worth preserving. It may be, though, that while one person begins to experience a considerable change of attitude the other continues to dwell on the old patterns of disagreement. This is a fluctuating period of relief mixed with doubts and anxieties and brings up many added worries at the same time: the practical ones of money; where to live; concern about children as well as the continuing turmoil over the relationship. For both the partner who moves out and the one who stays at home there may be many new anxieties to add to those about the relationship.

This may be one of the toughest periods of your life, whether the separation is temporary or permanent. Feelings of guilt, depression and vulnerability arise which involve your whole being and can lead some people into reactions such as withdrawal or frantic socialising. For some it is a traumatic period of pure survival. These feelings are experienced by many people who go through divorce. They affect some more profoundly than others so that each person has to find their own way through. Within your daily activities and social life you may have a deep sense of being alone. Though these feelings may be intermittent this makes them no less hard to bear, yet they can have a purpose. Learning to stand alone touches our greatest vulnerabilities but can also reach an inner strength which is in each of us. This involves our ability to understand what is exposed in us by the experience of divorce, and to achieve greater security in these untouched aspects of our individuality.

We become not only stronger within ourselves but the experience can be the foundation for new relationships.

All the difficulties we have been talking about in this chapter may appear at times so insurmountable that you seem to be getting nowhere. There may be moments of great happiness and freedom—perhaps for the first time in years—but also days of deep despair, loneliness, regret and even panic. But gradually as time passes you begin to feel a person again. Your "progress" depends on how much you are able to resolve both the practical difficulties and the emotional conflicts within yourself. A great many people go through a long heart-searching phase extending from before separation to beyond divorce which may last for a period of several years.

Sharing the difficulties of separation and divorce with others can help to provide a route through them but often it makes sense to seek professional help. Marriage problems can be explored and dealt with in talks with a trained counsellor or psychologist. This provides a sounding board for your feelings, helps to identify the areas that need to be looked at, and shows that there may be other ways of living with changing conditions. This is usually not an easy process but, looking at the positive side, to take this step can completely change your perspective.★

Some of the biggest problems of divorce arise directly from the haphazard and uncaring way in which many break-ups occur. You can still do what needs to be done yet in a better way which minimises as far as you can the inevitable upset and upheaval. For example, it is unkind to leave a partner just before Christmas unless there is no other course to take. Similarly, to go shortly before a family holiday which children have been looking forward to only creates additional upset. This is different from simply putting off the actual moment of leaving. If you have resolved to go and have made this clear then, in one sense, the pressure is relieved and you can try to time the event to suit the circumstances. One wife considered her husband's

★ There are individuals and a number of organisations who do this work, although it will not suit everyone. We say more about this in the chapter on the Professionals and there is a list of organisations in the Appendix.

position as a public figure and realised it would be kinder to wait and leave him at the end of his year in office as president of a society important to him. She told him she would continue to live with him until this period ended, to give him time to adjust, and for nine or ten months continued to accompany him to his society's functions as she had done before.

One of the most difficult phases when two people separate and divorce is to loosen the emotional bonds with the partner. Though physically living apart, it can take a long time to establish emotionally separate lives. This important transition may not be complete at a time when you begin to live with someone else. It is "work" which still needs to be done because the bonds linger and cannot simply be cut without repercussions. This enables you to separate in the true sense and continue to build, with your separated partner and children, a very different long-term relationship.

All sorts of subtle dependencies will have been built up when you have lived with someone for a long time and these have to be let go, even though the pattern of contact with the partner after separation varies considerably. Small things can assume greater importance than they would otherwise. To take one example, in all relationships there is a reciprocal set of household tasks divided between both partners—decorating, cooking, gardening, fixing the car and so on. Separation involves breaking this particular pattern and perhaps learning how to do some jobs you did not attempt before. This is often a gradual process which can take several years. One way of helping to make this change, which some people adopt, is to pick the right moment to ask their partner how to do a particular job, or alternatively offer to show them, or a friend may help. This is all part of establishing a post-separation relationship. One woman, on leaving, attached notes to various kitchen gadgets to aid a particularly impractical husband. If you don't know how to change a fuse or wash your own clothes properly you could find out.

However, there is a danger in asking for help from your partner all the time or in offering too much to them. Because money is usually short at this time it is tempting to have too much contact, which could be misinterpreted; it may be a double message that you don't really want to go. Some people will take any attempt to help as a sign that you will go back. Continuing ties of this kind make it difficult to free yourself finally from the marriage at an emotional level. The kind of help you give or ask for, if it continues, needs to reach the point where it is on a friendly basis, as with any other friend, and without emotional overtones. There is yet another reason why these ties have to be released. Unless this change is completed they will colour and interfere with any new relationship. Without gaining a measure of your separateness and identity you may relive the old relationship within new ones and so undermine them.

The experience of marriage or marriage break-up that some people go through affects them so deeply that the emotional pain can become a kind of paralysis. Their feelings may be so badly affected that they find it almost impossible to trust anyone afterwards and they may withdraw into themselves and shut off new relationships. Regret and bitterness are normal after such an experience, especially if you are now in difficult circumstances as a result. A period of withdrawal can allow a healing process to occur. The danger is that regret, bitterness and withdrawal can harden into permanent attitudes of distrust which undermine every aspect of your life. However, the "new start" that people often want after a very bad experience can come from within the experience itself.

Every marriage crisis emphasises fundamental differences between the two partners involved. Sometimes these take the form of marked personality traits in one or both which become exaggerated to the extent that they are the crucial factor in the continuance of the relationship. In many cases they progressively undermine the relationship until its inevitable destruction. These personality problems are emotionally very draining and can be extremely difficult to deal with. This is because they make it hard for the relationship to function from day to day and, secondly, because they are a product of the particular personalities of both people. These problems are complex and include, for example, explosive temper, constant deceit and extreme selfishness, heavy drinking, gambling, drug addiction, violence, promiscuity and combinations of these behaviour patterns. The deep anguish and perhaps fear these problems generate can make the other partner feel helpless and powerless. These problems can be so deep-seated that you may require professional help to find ways to resolve them. The danger is to leave things too long. However, if you are suffering, or have suffered, we want to point to some ways of coping which, we believe, can help you ease the situation.

First, part of the build-up to these problems is that when you were attracted to your partner originally, you were also drawn at an unconscious level to some of their unattractive qualities. They made a similar "choice". The powerful, even obsessive, attraction which two people feel for each other at first, and sometimes continue to feel, can obscure the necessary adjustments which have to be made to put the relationship on a more reliable basis—or to "withdraw the projection" to use the psychological term.

It may take a very traumatic experience to shatter the illusion. A woman who found herself in a violent marriage said she genuinely believed that things would return to normal and they would live happily ever after. "The point was that I still loved and cared for him desperately. It wasn't until I wound up in hospital for three weeks I realised I was wrong."*

Violence in marriage brings up special problems because events can reach a very dangerous stage before one or both partners decide to make any change, or decide to leave. Violence can range from an occasional blow in anger to regular physical assault. When a relationship starts to go wrong, because men are usually stronger and more forceful than women, the aggression that is within them can turn into a behaviour pattern where blows and fights take over. Less commonly, a woman may be the more forceful partner and a similar problem can arise. Two very strong-minded partners match each other in their aggression. The actions of both the "aggressive and the passive" partners may well have their roots in childhood so that old

* *The Guardian*, November 10, 1982

patterns and frustrations are being played out. For both partners their energy is being expressed in a distorted way. In the case of the "aggressive" partner, it is unchannelled and so not used constructively, while the "passive" partner is denying their assertive qualities and so failing to stand up for themselves. What we have here is a psychological vacuum in which the "passive" partner allows the "aggressive" one to act out their innate assertive qualities.

Continuing violence at some point forces a choice as to whether to live with it, with the obvious physical risks, or to try to change the situation by leaving or by looking for a way to improve matters, for example. You may already have decided you must leave out of sheer desperation and not knowing what else to do. However, violence can stem from a gradual change of a personality leading to illness. Small changes in behaviour in the relationship can build up, hardly noticed, to the point that something has to be done. The sensible first step is to establish that there is no illness, hereditary or otherwise, behind the outbursts. There is a whole range of conditions from hormonal imbalance to more rare diseases affecting the brain which can cause irrational and violent behaviour although it is more likely to result from personality differences. It is a harrowing and frightening experience to live with someone acting like this to the extent that you do not know what they may say or do next. It is also very hard to know what to do to alter the situation, especially if you do not want to admit to other people that you are being assaulted. You may become so desperate at this stage that you consider calling the police, or a neighbour may do so. Unfortunately the police are usually of only limited help. Their normal policy is not to interfere in a domestic dispute unless a crime is committed and in practice this means they will rarely cross the doorstep to intervene.

Here are some further steps you can take. First, if you have an understanding relative on either side of the family, sharing the problem with them might produce a way of dealing with it. One result could be that you discover some relevant, perhaps upsetting, information about your partner's background which you ought to know. For example, some people keep a previous relationship or traumatic experience as a closed book in their life. This is often a key to their present behaviour and can help you to understand it better. Some people have a special relationship with a particular relative who can talk frankly to them where a marriage partner may be unable to. This in itself may not solve anything but can provide some support where a partner is behaving unreasonably.

If your partner accepts that illness may lie behind their behaviour he or she may see their doctor. More likely they will not admit that they need help and their own state of mind often makes it impossible for them to recognise their problem. They might acknowledge that something is wrong but need persuading to seek help. At this point they could agree to go with you to see a doctor. If they refuse you could talk to the doctor yourself. In the very worst case your doctor may feel it necessary to commit your partner for treatment.

Where it is obvious that your partner is simply behaving badly and not taking responsibility for their actions, you must attempt to put this across to them. Many people will not face up to this side of themselves while few of those involved with them have the experience to deal with this situation. If your violent partner feels sorry afterwards and regrets what has happened you may be able to use this opportunity to persuade them to talk to someone about their behaviour, whether a doctor, counsellor or minister. Realistically, they may refuse to see anybody and even if they do, may refuse to look into their part of the problem. Some violent people will not discuss anything and here you must decide for yourself the limits of behaviour you are prepared to tolerate. How you spell this out is something only you can decide. A strong statement may produce little response, some communication may open up, or it may result in more violence. But tread carefully. An ultimatum made hastily can create more difficulties.

In the extreme, if the physical danger becomes too great to endure any longer, you may simply have to pack your bags and go. It is the act of doing what you probably realised has been necessary for a long time. Even this needs to be thought out so that legal problems can be anticipated, and a visit to a solicitor first is a wise precaution. If you are a woman and there is nowhere else to go, one of the women's refuges* will take you and your children for a period and provide support while you make new plans. Let a few friends and relatives that you trust know where you are.

Another approach in coping with violence is to consider your own behaviour. Many of us learn ways of expressing ourselves which unconsciously signal things to others we do not intend. This can be both through what is said and our "body language". The tone of voice and even the gestures you use could be producing angry reactions from your partner. This can even start from a single careless remark during conversation. Someone who is hypersensitive to any apparent criticism can react to almost anything you say and treat even an innocent remark as a personal attack. In an argument blind rage can be provoked in someone by dragging up old grievances instead of sticking to the point at issue. Provocative statements, or sarcastic remarks which are intended to wound and destroy a person's self-esteem, can have the same effect.

We are not always aware of this effect of our words on others and we can be provocative without realising it. Much depends on the personality of the person we are talking to and even a mild person can be provoked eventually. Try to understand how your partner experiences your remarks and see if you need to modify your approach. You may need to ask directly sometimes to find this out.

A marked difference in the strength of two personalities may itself contribute to a violent relationship. In this case the violent person may be preying on a weak and unassertive partner. The mild person who would do anything to avoid a scene is, we suggest, not putting any limits on their partner's behaviour from the very beginning. Their own powers of assertion remain unused while allowing their aggressive partner at the opposite end of the scale to do as they wish. In this way it can be said that the victim of the violence unconsciously attracts it. This interaction of opposites is bound to continue unless some change takes place. This usually demands that the passive

* See *Women's Aid* in list of organisations.

106

partner starts to assert themself to gain a better balanced relationship. In practice, perhaps, the only way that she (or he) can safely assert herself (himself) at this stage is to leave the relationship and this very act may be what the situation demands of them.

It may be hard to accept that a violent partner cannot change but by trying to adjust your own attitude to take some control you start to deal with the situation at another level. For some women in this position, to leave such a relationship can be the first really assertive act in their lives. Kaleghl Quinn, in her book on self-preservation for women* points out that those who have inner strength and a feeling of self-worth give off a sense of harmony and so minimise their chances of becoming the victim of a street attack, while those who don't are liable to attack. It seems likely that the same mechanism is at work in marriage: that a woman who is confident and assertive is unlikely to meet violence from her marriage partner while the unassertive woman with unexpressed drive may attract one with violent tendencies that are acted out.

An attack in the street and violence in the home can be seen as close parallels, and that staying in a violent marriage is in part a passive choice. As Kaleghl Quinn says, women feel very reluctant to abandon the passive female role, even to the extent of feeling sorry for the man who attacks them. She points out that women absorb the general idea that they are "not important enough to have the *right* to be angry" about the way they are treated.

Anger is part of the normal range of emotions and it is necessary to get angry about such a situation to make any changes. Most of the same things can be said about the man who is dominated and abused by his wife. A lack of any real assertion only invites the complete opposite attitude to emerge in a partner.

A relationship in which one partner has a serious drink or drugs problem raises intense difficulties. Where do you finally draw the line and take active steps to re-establish or sever the relationship? How do you come to terms with leaving the

* *Stand Your Ground: A Woman's Guide to Self Preservation* (Orbis)

person you love? These are difficult questions to answer. A person who has been taken over by compulsive behaviour of this kind has lost not only their sense of themselves but also most of their ability to function within the relationship. Further, the behaviour itself dominates it.

Because this involves both partners or the whole family, the very difficulties this raises can mask the underlying personality blocks within the individual concerned. Identity problems, attention-seeking, the desire to escape from a harsh world, and other factors are among the possible causes of this behaviour pattern. However, these real causes may never emerge or be uncovered in the course of any treatment, so that the individual's partner remains enmeshed in a twofold trap. There are practical difficulties and emotional draining that go with living with someone who may have the needs of a child. Further, there is the unconscious attachment between the two partners in which the caring and compassion of one is exploited by the other. This unequal relationship is closer to that of a parent and child than two adults in a mature partnership.

The love which the "parent" partner has for the "child" holds them as the victim of the situation because to consider doing less for them, or want to abandon them, immediately raises guilty feelings. This perpetuates the situation. The caring here is all one way but caring also means caring for oneself. By doing too much for your partner you deny them the necessary space to take responsibility for caring for themselves.

Appalling dilemmas of this kind are easy to discuss when they occur in other people's relationships, but for a person living through this experience the choices look bleak. The impossibility of being able to do anything which improves the situation is depressing and very upsetting. The sense of helplessness only reinforces these feelings so that the spiral always seems to lead downwards. The urge to leave can be overwhelming yet seem wrong. Years of conditioning hold us in attitudes of staying the "good" wife or husband, of fearing disapproval by parents or friends, or simply thinking "I couldn't do such a thing". Even set ideas about the idea of "failure" in marriage make it hard to look beyond the guilt feelings.

However, an extreme situation of the kind we have discussed demands that you face it, become aware of the options, and treat them as choices you can make. To do this will involve stating for yourself and then to your partner what you need, which requires assertion, courage and tact. Remember, any decisions you make or fail to make, affect the lives of children and others who may have no power to make such decisions for themselves. Caring for oneself is as important as caring for others because it involves taking responsibility for your own life and the lives of those you love. It can be part of a process of self-discovery to realise gradually that you may be pouring enormous concern and energy into a bottomless pit.

This leaves you very little choice but to make some very definite decisions. The more difficult a person becomes, the harder it is to reach any agreement with them. With some people you simply cannot get through to them. Or it may be that you have both reached a complete impasse. It is only when this is acknowledged that you can begin to shed the false hopes, and the pointless making up, and plan for your own and your children's future. For example, you can put to your partner some demands that, if met, will enable the relationship to function. At the same time you can make it clear that without this you plan to leave the relationship, either temporarily or permanently. Such an ultimatum may be a considerable shock to your partner, or they may take it as an idle threat, especially if such "conditions" have been made before. This time you must not go back on your resolve but do be prepared for emotional upsets which may follow.

Determination of this kind can arouse a number of reactions in a partner. Their behaviour may worsen or they may be resigned to your decision but it is extremely difficult to predict which way events will go. They should at least know where they now stand and thus you will too; in itself a step forward that takes off some of the pressure. One husband who told his partner firmly, after many violent arguments, that he was moving out for good, found at first he was not believed. When it became obvious that it was meant the atmosphere cleared and the decision became accepted. By the time he left three months later both were able to discuss calmly the arrangements that needed to be made.

This setting of definite limits to your partner's behaviour and perhaps your own, is the crucial issue. It is a matter of cutting through preconceived attitudes and reaching the essentials of the relationship. This spirit of changing attitudes is a very positive way of gaining strength to move on, rebuild your life and avoid the trap of being a victim of this relationship and perhaps any that follow.

Many of the suggestions we have made in this chapter demand consideration, flexibility and concern for other people's feelings. This is not easy to achieve, particularly at a time when your own feelings may be confused. Yet there is a balance which can be reached which creates a positive pattern for your life in the years ahead. Others have achieved it—so can you.

CHAPTER 6

Professionals

In any marriage break-up the situation will eventually develop from being contained within the circle of home, family and friends to reach other areas where professional people and agencies become involved. This is a particularly sensitive and painful period since you may have to talk about very personal parts of your life to outsiders. Over a period these may include a solicitor, doctor, counsellor, bank manager and accountant; and might also extend to your church minister, the courts and associated social agencies.

The point at which this happens, and how, is a keynote to the way a separation and divorce is handled, and while for most people it is random and largely out of their control, it does not have to be. Linda was devastated when John told her he had been having an affair and was going to leave. She became desperate when he moved in with his girlfriend. Friends and family support did not help and she went to her doctor who prescribed anti-depressants. These were of little comfort and in the depths of unhappiness Linda rang the Samaritans a number of times over the next few months until she eventually found herself on a more even keel.

In contrast, Margaret and Dick had been getting on badly for some time when Dick left suddenly after a huge row. Margaret, extremely upset and in a state of emotional shock, had to cope with their three children. A neighbour suggested that she and Dick could try getting help with their problems at a family counselling agency. Dick was almost contemptuous at first when Margaret asked if he would go, but he eventually agreed. Though living apart, they went to weekly sessions at the agency for more than a year, working on their problems together with two counsellors. They divorced eventually, but in the process they came to respect each other more as individuals and learned much about themselves.

In the first example professional people became involved only as a desperate last resort. The second couple were able to make a positive decision to get help to try to sort things out and this minimised the lingering upset the separation caused.

There cannot be a prescribed route or method which every couple can follow to handle their break-up, but this chapter is devoted to the idea that in many circumstances professional help of some kind in the early stages, at the right time, can give two partners the knowledge to handle the situation in the most positive light possible.

The aim of this chapter is to offer a problem-solving approach to the situation in which you find yourself, whether in advance of a break-up, during it or afterwards, and one which is likely to produce benefits all round. This should be true whether or not your partner co-operates or takes any interest, and regardless of what terms you are on. The outcome, if you use the professionals wisely, is that if you do separate permanently, you are likely to be more able to work constructively and support your children through this traumatic experience, and this approach could not only be of benefit to you, but may also help your partner.

Doctors

The family doctor is often the first person to know that there are difficulties in a marriage—even before the partners or their families acknowledge it themselves. This is because doctors see many patients with complaints which they know from experience are signs and symptoms of unhappiness of some kind. There is an increasing awareness among doctors that physical and emotional conditions have to be treated very much as a part of a patient's total health picture, so they may take considerable pains to try to reach the root of the problem if the patient is receptive. How should you approach your doctor and what should you expect?

It is as much a part of the doctor's job to discover if there are emotional problems to be "treated" as physical ones and he or she could be a very helpful first person to talk to if you find that marriage problems are becoming difficult to handle. Unfortunately, various factors work against this whole person approach in many surgeries. Because the emphasis in medical training is on a physical cause for illness, many doctors are not taught that relationship problems (and indeed other types of problems) can manifest themselves in the form of an illness. Secondly, nearly all general practitioners are very busy, with many patients in their waiting room, and one way they cope with the system is by holding short consultations and relying on prescriptions for drugs as the major "cure". The personality of your doctor is also important. Male doctors, for example, often ignore the emotional component.

You may go to your doctor for the first time with a specific physical complaint or perhaps a condition that might have been troubling you for some time. You may feel that your complaint is linked to your marriage relationship.

If so, try raising the subject and see what he or she suggests. They may be willing to talk then, or make a later appointment to see you when there is more time, or perhaps they may suggest a counselling agency where you can talk with someone. Some doctors, because of the interest they take in these matters, are well connected to those professionals from whom you might find further help, such as a counsellor, therapist or some suitable agency.

Your doctor might offer to speak to your partner, either alone or with you both together. Although it is not common, a number of practices now have a counsellor attached who is a specialist in dealing with the emotional side of any illness.

We are brought up to expect the doctor to take our burdens from us and give us pills to solve our problems. In an extreme situation pills can be a useful part of the total help offered. The doctor may offer them to you for a short period. Beware of being offered them for an indefinite time, especially if your problems have not been brought out fully into the open.

A further difficulty you might encounter is that the personal values of the doctor could intervene. In some cases he may make moral judgments about you or your situation which are upsetting and do not help. If you feel that for this or any other reason you are not being given sufficient help you must seek out another more suitable doctor. You could try a different doctor in the practice or ask your friends if they can recommend one with whom you might find appropriate help.

The Clergy

The clergy fall into a similar category to doctors. Without having to put up a notice on their door saying "Marriage Guidance", they often find themselves approached by people for help with their marriage problems. Religious people are obviously more likely to think of talking to their local minister. Indeed, he may be the one person whom, if you have strong beliefs, are diffident, or embarrassed, you would trust in such circumstances.

Ministers can be remarkably sympathetic, with a wisdom which comes from dealing with conflicts of the heart and mind. Like the best doctors, some Ministers have great empathy—a gift for understanding what a person is going through. Many have an openness and understanding of human nature which enables them to offer much compassion to someone who is upset or in a dilemma. These individuals—in spite of difficulties of doctrine within the various churches—can give you a sense of guidance which helps you find your own personal way forward.

Whether you would want to approach a Minister about your marriage difficulties is likely to depend on your religious convictions, and, indeed, these convictions may make you ashamed or guilty about airing the subject anyway. Whether or not religiously committed, you can go through agonies of guilt about the idea of divorce, or a marital indiscretion, but a practising communicant may find the burden intolerable. A lifetime's vow to live with someone is a commitment you may feel strongly cannot be broken, but equally you feel it cannot continue, so what do you do? One answer we suggest is to try not to grapple with too many absolutes at once. Initially, it is better to test the water—to accept the fact honestly that you are in a kind of limbo about your marriage and that you have to find the next step for yourself. You can do this by sharing your feelings, preferably with your partner but at least with a sympathetic person who will listen but not judge. It is not for you to judge either, at this stage. What you need is more information about the situation and the feelings involved, particularly your own, and a Minister who is able to allow you this is of tremendous support. This period could take months since you need time to reflect before taking any decision. One problem here is a risk of identifying too strongly with your own beliefs and opinions; they may be too narrow to deal with the dilemma. If your inner feelings point towards a separation or divorce this need not deny a continuing concern for your partner's welfare. Anything you now feel or do is not helped by any judgment by anyone of what is "right" or "wrong". What is important is that you are open and honest with yourself and with others.

The sanctity of marriage is a fundamental concept, but it is also necessary to consider that change does occur in life, and this may force a person to examine whether a partnership must change with it. There are Ministers for whom this approach is too threatening, touching personal insecurities behind their firm convictions. Some intimate areas of relationships may be difficult for some clergy, and other professionals, to discuss if they hold closed attitudes. To raise your doubts in the first instance with someone like this who finds safety in dogmatic assertions that leave little room for the wider realities of life, could divert your efforts to find a solution. This might create a situation where you are effectively discouraged from working through all these feelings. Other sections in this chapter may help you for there are always different approaches to consider.

Counselling

In dealing with your particular problems you have to ask yourself some difficult questions: Do I want to improve the situation, or can it not be repaired? Am I being irresponsible in wanting to leave my partner? Is there an alternative? What do I want that I don't care to admit? Do I want him/her to return? Am I also responsible for what has happened? Can I ever forgive them? How prepared am I to do whatever may be necessary to resolve things with the least damage and loss of respect to myself and others, especially my children?

This raises deep questions about what we want from life and the nature of our personalities that we have explored in earlier chapters and it takes us to the services offered by trained counsellors. Counselling, almost unheard of a few years ago, is a growing part of life these days. It offers a person or a couple a chance to explore with others trained to help the options at a critical time in their life; a time when the old ways of doing things seem not to work any more, or when a new situation appears such as marriage breakdown, bereavement or redundancy. It provides a framework in which you yourself can make decisions and move forward through acceptance of your feelings and acknowledgement of your identity. Do not expect direct advice. You may feel you want to be told what to do but this is not part of counselling because it is recognised that giving advice is not really a long-term solution. In contrast, conciliation is the means whereby a mediator helps a couple come to agreement on particular areas in dispute before a divorce is finalised. The most common issues are maintenance, custody and access.

The Marriage Guidance Council is perhaps the best-known counselling agency and since it is concerned with the relationship between a couple whether or not they are legally married, it is appropriate that we talk about this organisation first. The Council has been in existence since the 1930s when divorce was comparatively uncommon and also expensive. It was also very much frowned upon so that the climate in which the Council works has changed dramatically over the years. Contrary to the opinion many people have, the Council's aim is not necessarily reconciliation but is to help couples—whether or not they wish to stay together. The outcome is not pre-judged.

The counsellors will see you on your own or with your partner. Sometimes the work takes the form of helping people to cope with a change in lifestyle, or view of life, which has caused a rift; at other times it is to help find the most positive meaning and way forward for those in a marriage breakdown even if it cannot be healed or repaired. The Council operates in all of Britain's larger towns and therefore is accessible to most people in the country. Because it is concerned primarily with the quality of relationships, its counsellors will see anyone, married or single, who has a relationship problem they want to talk about. They will also help people with their emotional difficulties and any problem over money or with their children during and after divorce.

Throughout the country there are a number of organisations which provide help of a similar kind. The Westminster Pastoral Foundation will also work with a person singly, or with their partner, to reach some solution to their problems. The Foundation is based in London with affiliated centres in many parts of England including most major cities. Like those of the Marriage Guidance Council, its counsellors are people who have a strong combination of psychological insight and solid experience of the ups and downs of life. They are often mature people in their middle years to whom this kind of work is not a profession in the normal sense since they usually have come to it only as a result of their own experiences, and they may not work at it full-time.

In another category are the professional counsellors working at the Family Welfare Association which has offices in different parts of London. These are people who are likely to be social workers by training and part of their work is done through the counselling method. The association, as its name implies, is concerned with the general well-being of families, so there is an emphasis and particular concern with children in a marriage or similar relationship.

Counselling usually involves one person or a couple and one counsellor, but another approach is to have two counsellors working together with a couple. This has the advantage that each partner is "represented" by a counsellor and this helps where it is judged that one partner could feel that a single counsellor might take sides.

Among the wide responsibilities of the Probation Service is

that of helping with marriage difficulties. It is the only statutory body with this official responsibility. Courts have the help of probation officers who can be asked to explore the possibilities of conciliation or reconciliation. They can be asked to provide a welfare report on children in custody disputes. The service's increasing role in providing help is reflected in both its new divorce awareness courses and its involvement in the growing national network of conciliation services being co-ordinated by the National Family Conciliation Council. The awareness courses are open to both adults and children and deal directly with the emotional problems so that feelings such as anger, grief and sense of loss can be understood.

For those with particular religious or other beliefs two organisations providing counselling help are the Catholic Marriage Advisory Council and the Jewish Marriage Education Council. The Catholic Council has centres in many towns up and down the country; the Jewish Council has two centres—in London and Manchester. If you belong to one of the ethnic minority communities such as Indian, Chinese, Greek or Turkish, you may well need to search locally for social workers or counsellors who understand your value systems and beliefs surrounding marriage.

If you are particularly worried that your relationship is affecting your children, the Child Guidance Clinic can provide support and help for your children and yourself.

There are rarely instant answers in counselling and the work that these organisations do with a client usually continues over some weeks, months or even a year or two. It takes time because new ways of coping, or a profound change of view, are unlikely to materialise overnight. The entrenched habits and thought patterns of a lifetime do not yield easily to ideas of change, even necessary change, and the process requires patience on the part of both client and counsellor.

John was urged to go to the Marriage Guidance Council by his solicitor when he and Vikki decided to divorce after Vikki admitted that she had been having an affair for two years. John says: "For the first few sessions I kept saying, 'Vikki did this, Vikki did that and Vikki did so-and-so,' but I didn't talk about myself. Eventually I got round to discussing things that had not been right between us which I hadn't wanted to look at, and ways in which I had contributed to the situation."

Sometimes both partners will go to talk through the problem, sometimes only one will. "Vikki flatly refused to try it," John says, "and it is only now, three years after the divorce, that she can say, 'I realise now what you were getting at when you talked about some of the things that came up when you were in counselling.'"

You may find, if you do go for counselling, that you have to wait for an appointment but this varies from one organisation to another. Remember that a crisis is not always the best time to tackle the underlying problems which may have led up to it.

Whatever the outcome if you have counselling, it is likely that you will gain a greater understanding of what is happening in your life at this time—an understanding you might not have gained otherwise.

Psychotherapy

For any crisis in life, support of some kind is needed, whether it is just to be touched or held, be given a place to stay, provided with a meal, or to share some understanding by talking it through. In marriage breakdown, one means of support which you may find you need is psychotherapy. This goes deeper and sometimes beyond the ways in which counselling may help, by exploring the personality further to create understanding and self-awareness. Psychotherapy is not necessarily required when a relationship breaks down but for some people it is a key to aspects of themselves where some beneficial change can take place.

The word psychotherapy may immediately throw up an image of classical Freudian psychoanalysis with deep probing of the mind over several years. This kind is expensive and only useful for a few. Psychotherapy is an umbrella term for a wide range of approaches using different methods. Of these, one or several may be helpful to any particular person. They have in common the helping of the mind and emotions without drugs to enable people to understand themselves better. The techniques may include hypnosis, transactional analysis, meditation, visualisation, cognitive therapy, dream interpretation and group or family therapy.

Of these one increasingly used method is visualisation, in which a person is encouraged to allow his mind to produce an image which can be interpreted and shed light on some aspect of himself or the situation he is in. Hypnosis is extremely useful in releasing tensions from the past and is also used to resolve personality difficulties. A therapist may help a person explore the meaning of particular dreams, which the unconscious produces as symbols to indicate attitudes of which the dreamer may be unaware. The unhelpful attitudes can be examined and changed and the positive ones acted upon. Often a client will be asked to draw a sketch of what he or she has been visualising or dreaming about and this brings further insights. Group support or family therapy involves working with a number of people where their personalities and various interactions are explored. In this way destructive patterns of individual or family behaviour can be faced and, in time, may be altered. The likelihood is that one basic approach will be offered, but some therapists are trained in several techniques and may use one or more as they feel appropriate and which the client is happy to work with.

Many therapists help their clients to consider attitudes and feelings which influence both behaviour and relationships. To do this it may be necessary to reach carefully back to adolescence or childhood to allow the client to re-experience and understand events and attitudes which still influence him or her in ways they are unaware of.

Time spent in psychotherapy can lead to various understandings of a marriage crisis, such as:

—acknowledging your own responsibility in the interaction with your partner
—allowing you to reach belief in yourself as an individual

—learning not to judge other people
—showing the value of listening
—indicating the importance of communicating and asking if you don't understand what is said to you
—opening private areas of thought that you may want to explore but cannot talk about elsewhere
—providing feedback on your attitudes to family and other relationships

Insights gained from work of this kind may not only help in specific ways but can be a rich experience. They can enable you to re-direct your energies and concentrate on what is necessary in your life.

Most of us want to talk about ourselves in some way, and usually feel able to do so, although we may not find it easy to discuss a problem with a therapist. Though you want to go, you may find a natural reaction against revealing personal details in the first session or two. Some of us for various reasons do not want to talk about ourselves, but nevertheless it may be useful to consider a therapist. Alternatively, assertiveness training or physical exercise, for example, may be more helpful. There is a strong element of release of inner tension in both approaches, and not everyone feels the need to delve into the past, be shown insights into their state of mind, explore their dreams or go through a year or two of classical psychoanalysis. The essential element is release in some way whether it frees anxiety, depression or personal conflicts.

The concept of psychotherapy is evolving all the time. Methods which are standard practice today often began as a radical idea, and new ones are likely to evolve. Doctors, psychologists and psychiatrists in the Health Service do use some of these techniques but they are mostly available privately. The idea of psychotherapy in some form and the name of someone who can help may be suggested to you by one of the professionals with whom you come in contact, such as your doctor or solicitor.

Because it is a wide field, a therapist is best found by recommendation, but it is worth trying to check as far as possible the reputation of anyone you go to. Psychotherapy can produce emotional and physical reactions which you need to work with and go through. These can include feeling drained, bouts of crying and aching muscles. Also there are feelings of well-being and joy. If you are in therapy you need to recognise for yourself whether a particular therapist or technique is suitable and whether you are benefitting from the work. Remember it is an active process with a two-way involvement and not a passive one such as taking prescribed drugs. If you have strong doubts, a *good* professional therapist will understand these feelings and not press you to go on. He or she will allow you to continue at your own pace, stop further therapy or find another therapist. A finishing point may suggest itself or a point may be reached where they suggest that you continue the work with someone different.

Some of these ideas may be unfamiliar to you but do try to be open-minded about the subject and put aside any preconceived views you may have. To see a therapist is not a sign of weakness nor a label of mental illness as some believe. It is a positive step that shows you are taking charge of your life and caring for yourself.

A therapist almost invariably has experienced therapy himself and has faced crisis in his own life. He is essentially a catalyst for your own change and not an authority figure or an "expert" who will tell you what to do. Some clients do try to rely heavily on their therapist, expecting them to give constant advice or carry their burdens. However, therapists are trained to watch for this and guide their clients towards what they must do for themselves. One specific danger is that people occasionally have unfortunate experiences with therapists who handle things badly. In the extreme this can lead to manipulation of a vulnerable person by a stronger one; though common sense will enable most people to steer clear of such individuals.

Don't expect quick results in the first few sessions since it may take this time to establish a rapport between you and to find out what the therapy should focus on. The outcome of the work will be worth it.

Choosing a Solicitor

The point at which you decide to consult a solicitor is a watershed in the process of getting divorced. There is no longer any doubt that you have taken the significant step that can be expected to resolve the situation. Until this time the intention, though real, remains for the majority just that.

The solicitor's part in the process can be a crucial one because he or she helps to set the whole tone of the divorce, which influences your future relationship with the person you are divorcing. A sweeping statement maybe, but it is true. In a situation which may be fraught demands considerable tact and sensitivity, and it is essential that your solicitor should act firmly but diplomatically. Letters have to be sent, requests made, a settlement worked out, perhaps with a partner who is distressed, vengeful or apathetic. The way that you and your solicitor *together* handle this can make a considerable difference to the outcome.

To take the worst case. You may be feeling angry with your partner, hardly speaking to them, and decide that you are not going to concede anything. They may be in a similar mood. You both may find solicitors who are prepared to write sharp, demanding letters to the other partner (but in fact the other solicitor since he has to deal with them) and for a fee each time, of course. Both sides can dig their heels in and the stage is set for a long and bitter battle which may last for long after the divorce is over. If you are in this frame of mind you may find that your solicitor will say that you are being unrealistic and decline to act for you.

The vital function a solicitor serves is that he will know your rights and those of your partner in your particular circumstances, and those of any children you both may have. The law is complex and changing, with many legal and financial pitfalls, and it is important to be aware of the rights that each of you has in order to gain a clear perspective on your position. A couple with no children conducting their own divorce can do it by themselves, but even here half-an-hour with separate solicitors will make sure that nothing has been left to chance, say if there is an agreement to divide the house and possessions.

If you have your own solicitor you may well want to see that person now. However, couples commonly have a solicitor who handles their joint affairs. In this case one of you will have to find another solicitor. In any case a solicitor has to be found, and sometimes quickly. But here the operative word is not "found" but "chosen". You *choose* a solicitor and by making a choice about the person who acts for you, you can ensure that as far as is possible you are being represented by someone providing the right kind of help and in whom you trust.

The best starting point, even before you look for a solicitor, is to consider what you want. Examine your feelings and state of mind as calmly as you can. You may be uncertain whether you want to divorce or not, but for now are more interested in settling the terms of separation. You may want instead to find out tentatively whether you have grounds for divorce and whether that is the best way to proceed. Or you may just want to get things over and done with. The most important thing is to be practical. No matter what your situation and your feelings about it, you need as simple and as sensible an arrangement as can be managed and you need someone who can help you achieve this despite, for most of us, the deep emotions which surface and upsets which occur during separation and divorce.

Not everyone who goes to a solicitor about divorce immediately begins divorce proceedings. It is his job to work for the best solution to the problem on your behalf and this might be a legal one, but he can act in other ways you might not expect. For example, he might feel that the situation between you and your partner has not yet reached the point where divorce proceedings are the next step and may advise you, or both of you, to think things over. He could suggest that you, or you and your partner, seek help of some kind such as counselling for your marriage problems. This may be because he believes that while divorce may be the answer in the end, a lot of issues could be straightened out first, so simplifying the process. Alternatively he might recommend that you both seek the help of a conciliation service to resolve particular problems that would otherwise complicate the divorce. Or there may not be reasons sufficient in law for divorce at this stage, say if you have just separated and there are no clear-cut grounds such as adultery, or unreasonable behaviour of a kind that makes it impossible for the marriage to continue.

A perceptive solicitor with good contacts could even suggest that some work with a therapist, perhaps to cope with depression, would be more useful to you than plunging straight into divorce proceedings, or would keep up your spirits while you start them. But it must be said that this comprehensive approach is still unusual and not what solicitors are trained for.

A good solicitor is patient, helpful, sympathetic and fair but not every solicitor acts in this way. Any profession is a microcosm of people at large and there are unfeeling solicitors who like to win court battles and to whom the letter of the law is of more importance than the rest of your life which you, not they, will have to live.

It is common, for example, for solicitors to assume on past experience that their client's partner is going to be trouble, and they may automatically expect this response from them. Your response to accusing letters from your partner's solicitors could become stereotyped too, so that events may develop out of all proportion to the real problems. Very often people do act in set ways and solicitors, who are busy people, have to act in the most expedient way possible in the circumstances. This may involve firm and perhaps specific action if they feel a client needs immediate protection.

This is why your solicitor's attitude is as important as your own. If he is understanding and relaxed yet businesslike, you have a much better chance of a positive outcome than if divorce, to him, is merely a bread and butter part of his practice. Try, therefore, to find out who the good solicitors are in your area by asking around. Ask friends who have divorced who they went to and compare their experiences. Ask at the Citizens Advice Bureau if they know local practices which specialise in divorce cases and have a reputation for dealing with them well. Your doctor or church minister may well keep one or two names handy.

It is usually assumed that any solicitor you see is the one who will act for you but you can use the initial meeting to make sure that his approach will suit you. You can judge this partly by his manner and by whether his proposals are appropriate. His response will vary according to what he feels needs to be done. He may say that you have grounds for divorce proceedings and suggest how to go about it; he may advise some immediate action in serious circumstances; or he might suggest that you do nothing for the time being, until your situation is clearer.

You can also say that you would like to be shown a copy of at least the first letter that your solicitor sends to your partner if he acts for you. You would want to see this so that you can be sure it does not say anything you did not intend. A solicitor should agree to this without question if it is made as a simple request, not a demand. Solicitors do not act of their own accord but act only on a client's instructions with their agreement.

Some solicitors make it a practice to settle queries and negotiate over the telephone directly with the other solicitor, and may also go to see them in person. Sometimes they will arrange a round-table meeting attended by both solicitors and their clients which can correct misunderstandings, save time and reduce the bill. We believe that these methods are extremely helpful and ought to be used more often. These are points you might raise at the initial meeting and it is on the basis of helpful answers to such questions that you can feel confident that the solicitor would act in your best long-term interests. It will also help you to know his attitude to your partner. One solicitor put it very well when he said: "I always have to pay attention to the basic requirements of the other party because this enables settlements to be reached more easily."

You could be feeling angry, hurt, tearful or depressed even if the break-up was two or three years back. But it is important that you collect yourself by this point and work out—if you haven't already—what you want to achieve. If you are unsure, try jotting down some thoughts and ideas in a notebook. This will clarify the approach you are taking and help you hold on to your most positive intentions when having discussions with your solicitor. It will also give you something on paper that you can refer to when you are there. It is essential in dealing with him to keep a sense of proportion right from the start—especially if you feel wronged and want redress. No matter how angry or upset you may be feeling, your solicitor needs your honest co-operation to get to the heart of the matter and to help you work out what is best to be done, and to make the choices—about money, access and so on—that you will have to make. You need to be as clear-headed as possible.

As well as dealing with your upset, your hurt or your resignation, remember that you have to make a "business arrangement" of some kind with your partner, as well as an emotional one, that will put your affairs in order as far as possible for the future. The way to do this is to put the effort in now and not waste it later in resentment in the years that follow a messy divorce. Work hard to arrange the best you can. It may not be ideal but work at it, settle for it and then get on with the rest of your life.

There are practical ways you can help your solicitor. The first is to tell him, factually, all that he needs to know. He is acting in your interests but to do so he will want to see the full picture—the overall situation between you and your partner. It is at the first meeting that trouble can be avoided because, if you present him with a highly coloured account which leaves out half the facts, the first letter he sends to your partner could well include distortions and untruths which set things off on the wrong foot. It may be difficult and painful to talk easily about what has happened but bear in mind that, while your divorce and its circumstances are very personal to you, your solicitor will have heard many similar stories so he will be able to maintain a factual approach which keeps things down to earth. There is no need to paint a particularly unpleasant picture of your partner, or yourself, as some people do. The facts speak for themselves and the more magnified they become, the less likely it is that things can be settled calmly. An out-of-control divorce is like a forest fire—it consumes everything in its path and is expensive. The obvious anxiety you may have about the outcome is understandable but try not to worry unduly. One solicitor said to his client: "Let me worry for you—that's what you're paying me for. When the time comes for you to worry I'll write and let you know."

One of the ways of using your solicitor's time and services most productively is to do as much of the groundwork with your partner as you can and take any agreement you reach to your solicitors for them to ratify. That way you can agree exactly what you want within reason but have the safeguard of legal advice so that what you agree on is legally sensible too, and without loopholes. This also makes sure that children are properly protected and that the divorce can go through the courts unhindered. If conducting your own undefended divorce, you can ask your solicitor to check through the documents for you.

There is nothing to stop you writing letters to your partner and phoning them and their solicitors to clarify points that need to be settled—if one or both of you has the confidence. By doing it this way time may be saved and unfriendly solicitors' letters landing on your door mat are kept to a minimum. However, anything you do agree should be reported back to your respective solicitors.

If your partner starts the proceedings, the first letter you receive from their solicitors may make statements about your conduct and the grounds for divorce which vary either from the facts as you know them or from what you both may have agreed. Resist the temptation to make a quick reply which you think will make you feel better; give yourself time to consider and then put things back on an even keel with a firm and constructive approach which will achieve results. Destructive statements only lead to a bitter stalemate. Here is one way in which a constructive result was achieved.

Roger and Jenny separated after many bitter rows and decided finally two years later to divorce. Each had had one or two other relationships in the meantime. Roger had promised to get the divorce moving but when he did not Jenny went to a solicitor first. The first letter Roger received gave him a shock. It declared that he had been living with someone else (which he hadn't) and that Jenny was being generous in not suing for divorce on the grounds of adultery. Roger, feeling that Jenny had probably played down their marital problems and played up his more recent sex life, sent back a factual letter acknowledging that they had planned to start proceedings but pointing out several things: that he and Jenny had agreed some time ago that two years' separation as a result of their incompatibility was the reason for divorce; that adultery was not a factor either way; and that he had not been living with anyone.

At the same time he sent a calm, handwritten note to Jenny, and posted a photo-copy to her solicitor, saying that he felt it important that they stick to their arrangement and divorce amicably without making things worse for the children by arguing about their behaviour *since* they had separated.

The effect of this action was that the solicitor wrote back hastily to withdraw the statement that Roger had been living with someone and agreed that the issue was clearly incompatibility and nothing else. Roger hoped that from then on they would be cautious about making any more inaccurate statements which might put him unjustifiably in a bad light. Next he drafted a longish typewritten letter setting out as fairly as he could a proposed divorce settlement which included how the children would be provided for; which bills he would pay in future and which bills he thought Jenny should pay; and how the house and contents eventually could be divided.

He took it to his solicitor who suggested some amendments; then Roger sent the draft to Jenny's solicitors (and a copy to Jenny with a handwritten covering note). They in turn sent him a reassuring reply saying they had talked again to their client and could see that nothing was in dispute and hoped a divorce could be arranged simply and without any great delay. Later, when Roger rang Jenny's solicitors to check some details, he found them very helpful. They willingly clarified a number of points over the phone in the weeks that followed. Further letters were few in number and quite brief. The effect of all this was that Jenny, who had become very upset as divorce loomed as a reality, found that her solicitors were well informed and able to help her promptly.

Roger and Jenny did not find this all easy. Several phone calls about the arrangements slipped into angry exchanges that repeated the pattern of their break-up. For both the divorce was part of a long and painful period of readjustment. But there was enough good will between them to enable the talking to continue. They managed to hold to their agreement that it was essential to sort things out as best they could for the sake of the children.

Despite the difficulties, this approach always stands a chance of success so long as at least one partner is prepared to be very patient and quietly determined despite further rows. These can even be expected while both practical and emotional issues remain unresolved. If one person perseveres in making this contact, however unpleasant it is, the less patient partner may learn to understand what the other person is trying to achieve.

An occasional exchange of letters between two people who are separated or divorcing, even if they cannot talk to each other, can be a useful way to keep events stable. If something has been agreed verbally, such as visiting arrangements for the children, to set this commitment down on paper will remind both partners of the progressive steps they are taking. This can save misunderstandings or denials later, particularly if each solicitor is sent a copy. Letters of this nature save time and money on the solicitors' bills and help to keep the divorce arrangements within the control of the partners. But they have to be worded tactfully and in a considerate tone. They should make offers, not demands, or confirm arrangements agreed. The object is to clarify, record and persuade but not to insist— your solicitor is better placed to do this if necessary.

Misunderstandings can arise if you both expect your solicitors to effectively produce a settlement themselves rather than act as intermediaries and advisors. Watch for events snowballing and remember that as the client you can set limits if this seems to be happening. Here is an example:

Paul made a settlement offer to Rosemary through his solicitor which she was advised was inadequate. After a series of letters passed between the lawyers Paul could see "that they were getting into a fight". He said, "When my solicitor told me he was sure the court would regard the offer as reasonable, I instructed him to stop writing any more letters since the legal bills were going to cost more than was in dispute. I explained to Rosemary what I had done and why, and eventually the court approved the original offer." Equally, a woman in this position might set the limits.

There are some very necessary distinctions to be drawn in the area of what you give and what you ask for when arranging a settlement. If you go for what is fair and can be seen to be fair, and do it in a measured way, it is going to be much more difficult for your partner's solicitor either to justify or to pursue an unreasonable course of action on their behalf. Indeed, he or she may well work to persuade them that they are not meeting you half way and therefore are wasting everybody's time. This may help to moderate demands which could otherwise result in protracted disputes or litigation. The art, though, is to establish for yourself, with the solicitor's help if you need it, what is reasonable and even more than reasonable in the circumstances and offer it to the other partner, as Roger and Paul did.

Your solicitor could point out, on the other hand, that you are giving up too much. It is easy for someone who feels guilty, for whatever reason, about the break-up of their marriage to concede possessions and rights which they feel they no longer deserve. This can lead to a lopsided settlement in which they take more than their share of "blame" for the divorce—which could be reflected in the grounds which are filed, in leaving all the furniture and in handing over other benefits in a way which leaves their partner feeling victorious. If you feel this way yourself your solicitor will almost certainly recommend a more realistic settlement. To give away too much probably reflects your attitude in the marriage and is not a good way to deal with guilt because it can make you feel angry and resentful in years to come. Another reason is that any future partner may also have to face the repercussions. For example, if you leave all the furniture behind, and you are not well off, they might be justifiably annoyed that you have made too little effort to provide for yourself in your new life. They may well not want to sit on the kitchen chairs from your old home but these can be sold. More important is that you begin to stand up for yourself—and are seen to be doing so.

Taking care of the future also means making a Will on getting divorced, or changing it if you have made one already. This is for the obvious reason that your life and your alliances are changed by the divorce. You are unlikely to want to leave everything to your ex-husband or ex-wife when you die, even if they have the children, and you might want to leave the children everything. You may have another person or a new family that should be accounted for in the future and you need to put all your affairs in sufficient order to save confusion or wrangles which might otherwise occur, perhaps years later. Remember also to tell those concerned that you have made a Will and where it is kept.

Many people get a very uncomfortable feeling about the idea of making their Will, and certainly to many healthy 30-year-olds it seems quite unnecessary. But it is wise to do so at this point. Treat it as "just business", something that needs to be done. Disputes over Wills, or lack of them, can divide families for generations and if you are getting divorced you have a responsibility to try not to leave a potential mess behind you when you die. If your families want to argue over what has been left to whom after you've gone, that's another matter, but at least you have made your wishes clear.

Money—You and Your Advisers

The way money is dealt with is important in any relationship since its use and the way a couple regards it says much about the values which are important to each of them. This is often highlighted in divorce.

Strong feelings are linked with money. If you believe your partner has treated you particularly badly, it is tempting to try to take him (or her) for all they have. A contract has been broken and your personal values may be linked closely to your income as a partnership. If you relate your own personal value to your financial position within a marriage, particularly where your partner earns the money, anger may take over when this changes. Similarly, for a person to have to pay out money in maintenance when their partner has left can rouse many bitter feelings which may only change when some understanding of their relationship has been reached. Counselling can help someone to cope with either of these attitudes.

Money is often used as a lever or a weapon to hold on to some control of a partner in an attempt to force them to pay literally for the upsets that they have caused. To act on these vengeful feelings might provide short-term gains but at the risk of prejudicing a realistic settlement which both will feel is fair. Men, through lack of knowledge, are often unaware of the share of their income which has to be spent on running the household. It is well to remember also that such feelings hide other attitudes, as the journalist Marjorie Proops says: "In marriage money is, perhaps, not so much an economic factor as an emotional one."* And in divorce too.

Sadly, some people will just not make the move from an unhappy marriage but stay in boredom rationalising this by saying to themselves: "I don't want my standard of living to drop so I will stay even though I really want to go." Others, probably through fear about money as much as jealousy, may say to their partner: "Why, if you're leaving, should I have a lesser standard of living just so you can have what you want?"

Financial difficulties can affect both men and women in different ways during separation and divorce. Men may be struggling to pay the rent of a room or flat and pay maintenance to a wife or ex-wife and children in the matrimonial home. Women may be struggling to survive on the maintenance they receive. It is often a matter of just not enough money to go round. To have to live on much less money than you are used to is very hard, especially if the necessities take all that is available so that there is nothing to spare for an evening out or a holiday. To accept financial help from the State can feel hurtful and raise feelings of being unable to manage. For those with higher incomes the difficulties will be perceived to be similar since it is the relative difference that is felt. In reality nearly everyone must expect to have a lower standard of living. In a study in the Social

* *The Marriage Minefield*, Daily Mirror, May 6, 1983

Sciences Research Council's Centre for Socio-legal Studies at Oxford, Mavis Maclean said that "many of the financial problems of divorced women did not relate to divorce but to problems all women faced—unequal pay and employment opportunities."*

To gain independence for oneself it is often necessary to gain control over money. For some women the lack of knowledge in areas of money management requires them to make a forward move. As we have mentioned elsewhere, it is now essential to learn the life-skills that you may not have attained in marriage.

At a very practical level, some of the initial help is likely to come from a bank manager. If you do not have a bank account, perhaps because your partner dealt with the family finances, you should seriously consider opening a bank account and explain your situation to the manager. He or she can advise on a whole range of services from a current account, through credit cards, revolving credit account, to borrowing money, insurance and advising on your Will. However, it is here that someone on a low income can meet difficulties. To obtain a credit card, for example, you will need £50 in your account which may be hard to find. But once you have a card it helps with spreading credit, although some people find them too great a temptation. You will need to consider if your circumstances make having a credit card a risk. A revolving credit account, which may go under other names, allows you to have credit of ten times an agreed monthly payment. For example, you can pay £30 per month and have credit up to £300. This may be more suitable than a credit card.

If you have a joint account with your partner, it is essential to judge when to close it to prevent any possible difficulties over one partner clearing the account. This does happen. A salary being paid directly into a joint bank account must also be altered and a new account opened. You can use the same bank since confidentiality is kept. You may prefer to move banks, however, if you do not want to meet your partner there accidentally, or are moving to another district. If you have no bank you could arrange appointments with several bank managers to find one who is understanding of your needs.

* *The Guardian*, September 3, 1982

134

At all stages of financial management, try to assess your needs and then make sure they are catered for. For women, this may mean fighting against the traditional patriarchal approach summed up admirably by one solicitor and pension expert when he said: "The trouble with the present way of looking at pensions is that actuaries who do the sums are trained to regard men and women as members of two distinct groups, instead of looking at their needs as individuals. . . The whole point about pensions or any kind of insurance is that people need protection. And these days it is quite clear that men and women need equal protection."★

Most of us are aware of the use of insurance for our cars and house and for holidays but how many of us bother to understand our national insurance contributions? These are compulsory contributions paid into a Government fund for the purpose of funding State services such as sickness or maternity benefit when you are away from work, and the State pension scheme. A lot of women who have not been working rely on receiving a state pension in old age based on their husband's insurance contributions. When you separate and divorce you must check your position carefully. Any woman who is divorced is entitled to a retirement pension at 60 depending on the number of years they were married in relation to the number of years their former husband has paid National Insurance contributions up to the date they were divorced. A wife's own contributions at any stage are also taken into account. For example, if a husband has contributed for 30 years and was married for 22 years, his ex-wife's pension basically would be 22/30ths of his. This basic pension can be altered by remarriage or your own contributions may give you a better pension by the time you retire.

If you have been paying the minimum contributions and then start to work for yourself or an employer, you will be liable to pay full National Insurance contributions in whichever class is applicable. Make sure you notify the appropriate authorities and start paying the full rate or you will begin to run up arrears. A big demand sent to you later will come as a nasty shock. For a

★ *The Times*, August 3, 1983

woman who is separated, other State benefits such as one-parent benefit and some other allowances can also be claimed. The whole area of national insurance and pensions is quite complicated and you must check with your local DHSS Office and Citizens Advice Bureau for details. It is up to you to find out and claim what you are due. In this as in other areas of financial matters do not expect any one person to have all the answers since you may have to talk to several people to take final decisions.

How you pay tax to the Inland Revenue will also change on separation and divorce. You will both need separate assessments. It is important to tell your tax office since on divorce a woman is eligible for both the wife's earned income allowance and the single person's allowance for the tax year in which she is separated. On divorce a man will revert to a single person's allowance and a woman also reverts to this allowance. It is important to check that the tax office gives the allowances you are due. You will also receive a new notice of coding if you have been working to enable the correct deductions to be made by your employer.

One key adviser for many people is an accountant. The more complicated your pattern of income and outgoings are, particularly if you are self-employed, the more necessary is an accountant. He or she will advise on your respective financial rights and obligations on divorce and how the law might apply in all areas of financial provision which includes maintenance payments, property adjustments and other settlements such as lump sums. Advice will be needed if, for example, you own more than one property or have school fees to pay. At a more simple level he will talk about your basic tax allowances, social security benefits that are applicable, mortgage repayments and the payment and receiving of maintenance in the context of the most tax-efficient way—your solicitor may have already touched on this. For a person to obtain tax relief on maintenance payments they must be made under a court order and not on a voluntary basis.

The higher your tax rate, the greater your tax relief and this is obtained through the PAYE code system unless you are self-employed. For amounts above the small maintenance payments of up to £33 a week or £143 a month to a wife, or the same for a child, tax relief at the basic rate is deducted first and any tax relief due for higher rates is obtained separately from the Inland Revenue. The person who received payment may have to pay tax on it and it is important to obtain a copy of the certificate of deduction of tax from your partner. Note too that any payment ordered to be paid *direct* to any child is taken as part of the income of the child who has a basic tax-free allowance like anyone else. If it is not ordered to be paid direct then the money is considered to be part of the wife's income. This is an important tax advantage to a wife and child (or children).

Taking care of all these aspects is an important part of your responsibilities. This will ensure your financial affairs are in good order so that you and your family are in the best possible position that can be achieved in the circumstances. More than this, it will enable you to become independent.

CHAPTER 7

Children

Your children are not your children
They are the sons and daughters of Life's
   longing for itself.
They come through you but not from you
And though they are with you, yet they belong
   not to you.
You may give them your love but not your thoughts,
For they have their own thoughts.
You may house their bodies but not their souls,
For their souls dwell in the house of tomorrow
   which you cannot visit, not even in your dreams.
You may strive to be like them, but seek not to
   make them like you.
For life goes not backward nor tarries with yesterday.

Kahlil Gibran

Every child is unique, and childhood is a stage in the development of an individual who is making his or her contribution to
the world from the moment they are born. Children therefore
are not, as many adults believe, a sort of junior species awaiting
adulthood before they need to be taken seriously. They are
already leading their lives. As Frances Wickes puts it: "We live
from the beginning; infancy is real life, not preparation for
life."*

Of course, each child has to be guided on their own route to
maturity. But even from a very young age they are individuals
whose own powers of discrimination and choice must be
encouraged and respected if they are to develop the true
confidence which comes from within.

To a child each day is special, a new adventure with new possibilities, and they can retain this freshness about life into adulthood
if they remain unhampered by their parents' problems.

* *The Inner World of Childhood* (Coventure, 1977)

Children like routine, but their openness generally enables them to welcome positive change when it comes and so they develop the experience which enables them to cope eventually with the variety and challenges of the adult world. But "upsetting" changes in their home life can easily affect their sense of security. Whatever the changes in their life, they depend on a strong underlying stability, whether there are two parents or only one. For these reasons children find difficulties and uncertainties between their parents profoundly worrying.

Young children pick up the emotional atmosphere at home and often "know" when something is wrong, even when nothing has been said. But they cannot easily interpret the verbal and visual clues which older children and adults might notice. This puts them at a serious disadvantage, leaving them worried and alarmed without being able to grasp the total situation.

The question, "Daddy, why don't you sleep with Mummy any more?" or, "Why does Daddy stay out so much?" may be the first of many worries in a child's mind. Or it may be that regular arguments in the home have created an atmosphere which has made him insecure and scared.

The many ways in which children react and suffer when their parents divorce are detailed in a close study of sixty American families over a five-year period by two child psychologists, Judith Wallerstein and Joan Kelly. They found, crucially, that children and adolescents alike experienced, "a heightened sense of their own vulnerability. Their assurance of continued nurturance and protection, which had been implicit in the intact family, had been breached. They confronted a world which suddenly appeared to have become less reliable, less predictable and less likely, in their view, to provide for their needs and expectations. Their fears were myriad ... but the anxiety itself was a widespread phenomenon."*

Children's reactions to stressful situations may not always be apparent or clear cut. Children are enormously resilient, even to the extent of accepting a parent's cruelty, but traumatic or continuing difficulties can seriously undermine their self-

* *Surviving the Break-up* (Grant McIntyre)

confidence and dull the vital spark which enables them to develop fully. One child will internalise its worries and hardly react when its parents are divided, and even make a concerted attempt to ignore what is happening, particularly if the parents are trying to do the same. Another may detach in a different but more positive way, by making a clear decision not to get involved, and for adolescent children this may be the only course they can manage.

Where there are several children it is often the most sensitive one who will react strongly. At school, temper tantrums, sulks and withdrawal, stealing, fighting, truancy and poor progress are all signs which can stem from a child's reactions to a troubled home life. This also includes parents' unspoken feelings and resentments. Two adults who are at war with each other, even if they rarely argue openly, may find their conflict acted out for them by their children.

Children behaving in this way can be highly disruptive at home or at school, or both, making their parents perplexed and angry. But this is really reactive behaviour which mirrors the prevailing situation. One boy, by the age of six, had come to ape the bickering relationship of his parents, continually losing his temper in the same way and even abusing them with some of the same acid comments that they made to each other. Their behaviour implanted a pattern in him which continued long after they were divorced.

The "naughty" child is bound to attract attention, but a child in similar circumstances who is not acting up may be equally affected. One who shows his emotions in a disruptive way is at least expressing them, however crudely; the "good" child who keeps his feelings bottled up may be just as much in need of help, but his need may not be apparent.

Children's greatest and most constant need as they grow up is security. It is the feeling of being safe, secure and loved which creates the foundations for their ability to make loving relationships in turn. When life between their parents is going badly they need a lot of reassurance; they need to know that they are still loved, that they are secure and that somehow the world is still the same as it was yesterday.

They also need information because sooner or later in any break-up a point is reached where the situation ought to be explained to the children, and this is often much earlier than when the parents get round to it. To take no account of this particular need amounts to a cover-up which breeds its own problems. It is at this point, ideally, that both parents should be able to decide together that they will be open and straightforward with the children when they are old enough to understand, and explain as much as necessary from then on. Often, though, this is not possible because the rift is too great, and where nothing can be agreed, it is then up to one of the parents to resolve to take the responsibility and this may well fall to you.

The right moment to explain the situation has to be judged but it is possible then to put things in the most helpful way possible in the circumstances—perhaps in separate discussions appropriate to children of differing ages. Ways of putting things positively are: "I'm sorry that Daddy and I are not getting on very well but we are trying to arrange it so that we will all be happier in future." Or, "Mummy has said she is going very soon to live somewhere else and she wants us to try to manage without her. I am sure that we can if we try very hard."

The words you choose are important. There is no harm in sharing your anxieties but there is no point in throwing in, for good measure, anger at your partner. Save that for other adults to hear. The emphasis is on keeping things low-key and on saying no more than the child can cope with at the time. If you are feeling very upset, then try to deal with the subject when you are calm enough to do so with some control. Children are usually sympathetic towards an upset parent but your aim, above all, is to hold their confidence in the future.

There is another reason for choosing your words with care. Remember that children can innocently pass on remarks made by one person about another and any criticisms of your partner that you share with your children could reach their ears. Children are naturally communicative and are far less tactful than adults who have learned diplomacy. The risk is that you could make things worse between you and your partner and that a difficult or volatile partner might use your comments as ammunition, or be tempted to use a child as a source of information about what you are thinking and doing. This can only put enormous pressure on a child. Finally, no matter how true, any adverse criticism of your partner will force a child to take sides for the wrong reasons, and this can have widespread repercussions.

For these reasons it is unwise to discuss sensitive matters in front of the children—even obliquely—believing that what they do not understand will not concern them. Until well into their teens children have yet to learn the subtleties of language, such as the use of irony, and they may treat what they hear literally or simply remain puzzled. Their lack of understanding will worry them more and may raise doubts which last for a surprisingly long time. Marion, now in her forties, recalls that as a child of about ten, her mother had many complicated family problems which were constantly being discussed regardless of whether or not she was present. "I couldn't understand much of what was said because I couldn't put all the words together and come up with their meaning. I felt very alarmed. It was not until years later that things dropped into place and I gradually understood. Even then it was such a relief simply to know."

There is nothing merely cosmetic in keeping low-key anything you say to your children. The most important reason is that it provides them with the space to form their own opinions—or withold them—so that they can find out for themselves what their feelings are. Remember that even in a divorce that is "friendly", the emotional strain for a child may be severe. The less you can tax children about the issues involved, the better.

Most children want to be "normal" with a Mum and Dad, even these days when they are getting used to the fact that children often only have one parent at home. Everything is magnified to children because of their lack of experience, and a large part of their everyday world disappears when a parent goes. One of the key people in their life who helps them, answers questions and knows them best, is no longer around. On an emotional level, a person who has loved them since they can remember has gone, and even if that parent was very lacking in love, they will be missed and the child will feel abandoned. On a deeper level, the child will no longer have both the masculine and feminine models—not roles—to relate to, so whole areas of experience provided by the parent who leaves are being "stolen" from the child—a huge gap that instinctively he cannot fail to register.

Where there is good warning that you are likely to separate, there is every opportunity to establish attitudes which will provide as much continuity for children as can be managed. To discuss the situation together and bring up—perhaps tentatively in the first place—the subject of what might happen and particularly how they will be cared for, provides some reassurance and gives children "permission" to say what they feel.

It is an alarming and sad prospect that a family will not be able to stay together and it is very hard to face this when it becomes likely. Adults and children alike get very used to the comfort and familiarity of everyday life and it is usually hard to accept the implications when all this changes, except in the most desperate circumstances. But if it has to happen, much can be preserved. There is no need for all that is familiar to be thrown aside. In fact your task, as parents, is to honour as far as possible the commitment you both made by having children. That commitment does not diminish as a result of separation and divorce; the problem is how to preserve it in the face of change.

Two partners who are still able to discuss matters can agree to continue to arrange things so that the children's lives are disrupted as little as circumstances will allow. A common practical problem is geographical; where will the partner who is moving out live, and will this be near enough for the children to visit? Some couples are able to arrange their lives so that they can continue to live comfortably in the same district, so that the children can walk or cycle the short distance between two homes. More often, though, it is not so easy. It may be necessary for the partner who moves out to take whatever accommodation they can find, even if it is miles away. Money may well dictate where they can afford to live and, for a variety of reasons, some people simply cannot cope with continuing to live in the same area as their partner after the break-up. And sometimes a man living apart from his family may take a new job a long distance away, feeling little need to stay in the same area as the children, and this may be the reason why he loses contact with them.

The important question is always whether the partner who leaves will be able to see the children often enough and it is here that things eventually can run remarkably smoothly if the parents have thoroughly prepared the way. Reassurance by both parents that the absent one will continue to see them regularly will go a long way to allay their fears. Children can be made to feel very much more secure if some of the usual domestic arrangements they are used to continue, such as one partner still collecting the child from school or after an after-hours activity; or a partner continuing the usual Saturday morning swimming lesson.

When separation does occur, children need to know what is going on so that they are not left with doubts or have surprise decisions sprung on them. In fact, what is to happen to the children needs to be considered from an early stage in the parents' decision to break up, not as an afterthought or part of some fixed plan. The selfish decisions which are often made, in which married couples or lovers keep long-laid plans and decisions from children until the very last minute, are evasive and sad and can only cause damage. To tell a child, as sometimes happens, that from next week they will be living with a new Dad or Mum they have never even met is little short of cruelty. Children need to know, at an appropriate moment, the answers to questions such as these:

Where are we going to live?
Who are we going to live with?
Where will Daddy/Mummy be?
Will I be able to see Daddy/Mummy?
What will happen about school?
Who will look after the dog?

Part of the responsibility of being a parent is to consider the answers to these questions long before the child has to ask them because this is essential to their security. In particular, it is nearly always a very good thing that children stay in the matrimonial home for a period at least, while their parents explore the long-term options.

Where a partner leaves suddenly with no warning there is no chance to prepare the children in advance for the changes to come. Yet either way there is an opportunity to handle the situation in the most tactful way you can devise, given some thought.

Where it is possible it is worth considering holding a family meeting with everyone present. Both parents can then explain to the children the details of what is to happen and answer any questions. This is useful even if one partner has already moved out and divorce proceedings are in progress. But it does rely on co-operation between the two partners and it may require fine judgment to gauge whether the meeting would be more upsetting than productive, or sabotaged by an unco-operative attitude.

One ex-husband who did persuade his partner that they should hold a meeting at the family home, once they had decided to divorce, is sure it helped to smooth things. "Miriam couldn't see at first why it was necessary but she agreed and we were able to say to the children we were divorcing because it was the best way everyone could be happy in future—and that we would still love them. I also wanted the fact of divorce aired with both of us present, so they could be reassured that we were acting together and considering them too."

Details like these can be arranged quite amicably but where the atmosphere is tense it may be necessary for you to "take charge" and spell out the priority you feel the children should be given. It may not be what you feel like doing; indeed your partner may not want to listen. But by taking charge you can accomplish a number of things. The most important is that you are taking an initiative which establishes priorities and shows that the children's welfare is paramount. By doing so you also establish that whatever you or your partner want, it has to be within the context of least damage to the children, not at the price of their happiness.

This raises the question of whether, provided the situation is not too difficult, it is worth remaining together for the sake of the children. Two people may accept that their relationship is not working but continue it nevertheless. Often, though, this is a one-sided arrangement where one partner quietly decides that they are prepared to stick things out until the children are through school. It is common for one or both partners to rationalise the situation in this way, but it is worth considering the implications: principally that this course of action resolves nothing. Whatever is at the root of the conflict remains simmering in the home during the years ahead, even and perhaps especially if both partners lead separate lives while sharing the same roof. While such an arrangement can last for many years, inevitably it is fragile. Something may occur to change it later and events then could be much more traumatic than sorting out the difficulties in the first place.

The majority of children don't naturally maintain long silences or bear grudges but if parents act in this way it poisons the atmosphere and their children start to withdraw. This is why two parents who decide openly or tacitly to stay together "for the sake of the children" when their relationship is in a mess may be doing more harm than good, while at the same time failing to resolve their own problems.

A vital question is whether this kind of agreement is truly in the children's interests. Often it is more to preserve things as they are and spare the parents' upset than to spare the children. But even where the family is kept together in this way it can create as much trouble as it tries to prevent, as Margaret's experience shows:

Margaret and David had gradually fallen out over a number of years until they found it hard to be polite to each other when they were both home. Sunday lunches with their two teenage children were tense and often unpleasant but as a mother Margaret felt duty-bound to stay even though she was, by now, a wife in little more than name.

Eventually the suppressed anger between them made its mark on Joe, the younger child, who began missing school because he felt unable to face lessons. Soon he was taking a week or more off at a time and eventually was hardly ever at school. Margaret, meanwhile, did the rounds of school specialists with Joe, arranged for home tutors and tried hard to find out what was "wrong" with him. In fact he was a sensitive child who had become caught up in the home's strong emotional undercurrents; he had lost the ability to learn and enjoy himself at school.

Young children often feel to blame for their parents' divorce because ideas build up in their minds which may be far from the truth. Therefore you must overcome, at this point, any reservations about giving the children a reasonably truthful account of what is going on and an explanation that things are going to change. They need reassurance that they are not responsible and this may well be important in clarifying the truth of their perception of the situation.

It is worth remembering too that older children are usually more acute than we realise and may already have perceived the truth of the situation that we deny. Wallerstein and Kelly, in their study, were surprised at the children's often realistic and sometimes sophisticated assessment of the causes of marital failure.

The final break can be planned in a variety of ways but there can be no fixed rules since every break-up is different. One wife agreed with her husband that she would leave, with the children, in a year's time after he had finished work on a demanding project which could not be disrupted—then moved, taking the children, straight into the house of the man she had decided to live with, whom the children had not met. This was taking a big risk but, luckily, the arrangement has worked so far. Despite this sudden introduction the children have adapted well and there have been no disputes with the former husband who has excellent access. This strong-minded approach can only work for those few with the intuitive judgment and confidence to carry it out.

The emotional reactions of children once the break has been made cannot be predicted with certainty. The transition to a new lifestyle demands care and tact, for children can easily feel that they have no say in their own lives. Snap decisions and sudden changes of home can make them fearful and upset in ways which may not show but make them suspicious of change in the future. If children have to move it is better if they are given a chance to become familiar with their new home before moving in, with a transition period in which they can use both. This is not always possible but the important element is that they are given some time to find their feet and get used to the new arrangements.

There can be benefits in a move too. Children will miss the absent parent but usually take to a new life where there are compensations. Rhona moved with her two young children to a house which was much nearer the shops and their school than their home on the outskirts of town. And the children's school friends were now within easy walking distance instead of a bus ride away.

Visits to the children at the family home by the absent parent can be traumatic for a period and may even be inadvisable. But providing there is no court order which forbids contact, there is nothing to stop a couple making whatever arrangements they can devise so that the children continue to see both parents.

For example, you may not be able to cope with going into the family home or having your partner walk into the house to collect the children but this is not essential. A push on the doorbell at an agreed time and they can be met at the doorstep with their coats on, while the parent at home can keep busy with a job upstairs. In any case, children often get used to looking out of the window at the due time and eventually come to the door by themselves. This way there is no need for the parents to meet while they cannot cope with it. But in time, any half-way system such as this may well lead to a cautious, but eventually friendly, meeting on the doorstep. If the atmosphere is still too tense for this, the children can be taken to a friend or neighbour by arrangement and collected from there and later delivered back. Responsible older children can make their own way to a neighbour's or be met in a public place such as a park or shopping precinct.

These ideas may sound makeshift but they can be made to work. They do, however, demand that parents set out to make continuity for the children the priority which overrides their wish to stay out of contact with each other. And they demand that agreements and arrangements made are stuck to so that children are ready and are met and returned at the agreed time. This is particularly important for younger children, who feel the most insecure; they need visits that are regular and to a timetable they can rely on. For a visiting parent to be late or change their mind and not come is very upsetting for a six-year-old who has been looking forward to it for days. Failure to be reliable and reasonably prompt alarms small children, annoys older ones and the parent at home, and can put the whole arrangement in jeopardy. If it is unavoidable that you have to change your plans to visit, *always* tell your partner in advance and the children if possible.

The key word is reliability. As we showed in earlier chapters, it may take time, tact and persistence to prove that such arrangements for access can work—that you can fulfil obligations despite the strain this may involve. By sticking to them as closely as possible the way is paved for more flexible arrangements at a later time; in fact as they get older children themselves become bored with the same fixed visits which make it hard to find anything new to do. Friends and hobbies become more important than parents as children grow up and this is a natural development in both divorced and non-divorced families. A visiting parent may feel rejected if a child does not want to see them on a particular day but this should not be taken personally.

The ideal, which many families reach, is that the arrangements eventually become completely negotiable, and are partly dictated by the children themselves—the complete opposite to the stultifying access times the courts will set for two parents still at loggerheads.

It is very difficult in practical terms to make a very cut and dried arrangement and this is, in any case, likely to conflict with the child's needs and what might suit the parents in future. A child may well take up an interest which involves spending a lot of time with the non-custodial parent or, conversely, may find so much to do with friends or the parent they live with that they are less interested in seeing the absent parent as frequently. Again this reflects situations which have parallels in ordinary family life. A child often relates much more strongly to one parent than the other and does more things with them. For example, a boy whose parents are married might spend a great deal of time doing woodwork and sports with his father. If his parents were divorced and the father lived elsewhere, the boy might prefer to spend a lot of spare time with him doing these things. We cannot emphasise strongly enough that this should be allowed for as far as possible and that fixed notions of access "every Saturday" or "every two weeks" cuts across the whole idea of a child having a say in choosing how he spends his time.

Parents usually regard access as the right to see their child but lawyer Jill Black points out in her book on divorce: "In fact, the courts look upon access as the right of the *child* rather than of the parent, which means that they approach every decision that has to be made about access by asking what is best for the child rather than what the parent would like."*

The law here is backing what is surely a child's fundamental need—to know their parents. And clearly this is a more constructive way for parents to see things too.

Access can also be granted to grandparents and even, in some cases, to aunts and uncles. In other words, there is a recognition that the child needs to continue well-established relationships with adults other than the parents—on both sides of the family—and these should not be denied. Where a parent strongly opposes any contact between the children and the absent parent this has a great deal to do, we believe, with an unconscious need to be with the child as well as feelings of resentment or revenge. A parent who has few interests outside the home tends to have a psychological dependence on keeping the child there. This is likely to be at the root of many battles over access though some undoubtedly are fought over the issue of which parent is the most suitable to bring up the child.

But keeping the children away from the partner has its dangers, and a child may be forced by an unaware single parent into the emotionally dangerous position of surrogate partner. In

* *Divorce: The Things You Thought You'd Never Need To Know* (Paperfronts)

their book Wallerstein and Kelly say that children put into this position began acting in disruptive, abusive and generally aggressive ways, often directed specifically at the mother. They "behaved like caricatures of jealous, domineering husbands" so that the mothers felt victimised. "Yet it was only when the mother was able to extricate herself from the victimisation and assert her adulthood that she was able to help both herself and her agitated child."

In contrast, the parent who has some absorbing interests will usually be happy to see the child spend time with the other parent—a healthier situation all round. Michael says: "When Carol and I split up she was determined that I should see the children only once a fortnight. But we talked it through and she could see that for me to see more of them would help us all to arrange a divorce settlement which allowed more flexible access. Now I can also ring her a few days ahead in the school holidays and say, 'Would they like to come on a train ride to the sea for the day?' and Carol is as pleased as they are."

Michael and Carol made sure that the wording on their divorce papers reflected this flexible arrangement and we feel that this kind of settlement is a positive use of the law. In other words, by making an agreement themselves, it wasn't left to the court to force rigid "visiting times" which at least one of them would have resented. This again shows the benefit of making the decision between you.

Under a free arrangement, once complete trust has been built up on both sides, visits can be fitted to the children's real lives in which, for example, youngsters get invitations to parties at short notice or become absorbed in a project they want to finish, as opposed to meeting the visiting parent at set times.

The whole problem of access after separation or divorce is very difficult for many parents, even where there may be little or no animosity. It is then that resentful wives may refuse husbands access to the children or make it difficult to visit, or a father may drift out of the lives of his children. In a survey, *Divided Children**, some of the parents with custody reported that they didn't mind that the absent parent no longer saw the

* Gingerbread, 1982

children, but other parents were certain that their children suffered because of the other parent's rejection of them. One person said: "In six years there has been no contact at all. I wish there was and so do the children (aged nine, ten and twelve). There have been no presents, no cards, no contact. The children feel hurt and rejected. They have happy memories of her but unless she sees them soon I feel they will resent her for leaving them."

Another parent in the survey said: "The children (aged eleven and twelve) often ask about their father. I don't know what to say. He lives only fifteen miles away but we haven't seen him for years. I've written to him but he doesn't reply. Perhaps he's moved. It's hard to tell the kids he's not interested."

The most heart-rending story we heard was of a couple who divorced and the father went to live with a woman whose garden backed on to the marital home. Once he had moved in he no longer acknowledged his children playing on the other side of the fence.

The emotional turmoil of having to establish a new life in difficult and perhaps distressing circumstances clearly can make people act in ways that are unfeeling or out of character. Not knowing how to act, feeling under pressure to act in certain ways, is common to many so that callous or indifferent behaviour may seem to have some justification. The urge to make a "clean break" and cut family ties is a tempting one but can never really be where children are involved. The idea of choosing to be no longer a part of a child's life has far-reaching implications. There is a big difference between the situation in which the absent parent no longer lives at home but maintains contact and one where he or she fades completely out of a child's life at an early age. Someone who, for whatever reason, never knew their father or mother, or has forgotten what they were like, may be left with a considerable problem which haunts their adult life. To lack direct knowledge of a natural parent creates a large gap in a child's certainty about himself and who he is. It also leaves him with an unsatisfied curiosity about what the parent was like. And it can result in a life's search to replace them—by marrying a "father" or "mother" figure, for example.

Parents are not necessarily in the best position to decide that their children no longer need them, or the parent who has left. Such a decision, which commonly isn't discussed, can be as much a means of avoiding more upset or be the outcome of resentment against the partner. Yet, as our examples suggest, it may be necessary to face and work through painful situations in order to avoid inflicting more distress on the children in the long term. As important, it enables two adults to continue the job of being parents.

It is denial of this basic need to relate which creates a void or a sense of loss that harms parents and children alike in the years to come. Nonetheless, the absent parent will sometimes get the feeling of being out of touch because their relationship with the children can rarely be the same as if they still lived with the children. This is difficult and inevitably these feelings will come and go but this is a part of divorce which has to be accepted.

Maintaining contact for the absent parent may be a difficult business, particularly where distance or an upsetting divorce make it hard to see the children. Unfortunately it is lack of regular contact which can have a pendulum effect, as for example with many fathers and some mothers, who become erratic in their concern for the children, and this may do more damage than good. Not to see the children for weeks then suddenly take them out to a restaurant and provide other treats cannot provide the balance they need. Similarly, the father who is not to be seen for months on end but then arrives with arms full of presents on Christmas Eve misses the point. In these circumstances children cannot relate to strangers, no matter how many presents they bring.

The biggest benefit you can give the children—and one which lasts them a lifetime—is eventually to reach an arrangement where the absent parent can meet the children in the custodial home in a friendly atmosphere. This may not be easy. The deep tensions, the mixture of guilt and anger, and the awful feeling in the pit of the stomach which may accompany many visits is horrible and upsetting. These feelings are so difficult to cope with that it is at this point many parents give up and the chance of creating a positive pattern for the children's future security slips away. You must be prepared for these upsets to reach what is important for the children; involvement with them in some of the everyday things of life which is crucial to their well-being—in non-divorced families too. Children want and need you to see little things like their new dress or toy, or something they have made, and this is easily done in the few minutes in which a parent calls to collect them. This is a direct and incalculable benefit reached by working through the difficult period. The unpleasant feelings of meeting like this in the family home will lessen in time where parents keep the goal ahead of them, and eventually everybody feels better as a result.

The idea—and indeed approval—of the "one-parent family" in many quarters relates to this problem of meeting amicably. The aim of independence and self-sufficiency after separation and divorce is a healthy one, for certainly a "new start" has to be made and years of marriage do make a lot of people too reliant on their partners. However, the label "one-parent family" also encourages some mistaken assumptions. One parent can certainly cope admirably and develop new strengths they would otherwise not have found. But this does not require that the absent parent should no longer be in evidence because one parent cannot take the place of two. Someone bringing up children on their own has difficult practical problems to resolve but there are dangers in identifying with this as a complete lifestyle in itself. Essentially, it is a transition period and by remaining open to the changes the family is going through, the possibility is allowed of a new "father" or "mother" coming into the family. To take on the whole burden and insist on bringing up the children as a one-parent family—as some embittered mothers and fathers do—is to deny them the balance two parents provide. Equally, the fact that many people find their independence only through divorcing and becoming a single parent makes its own comment on the problems of dependence in marriage. Similarly, professionals such as teachers and doctors may make assumptions about a child's difficulties which are based on preconceived ideas about one-parent families.

The problem of the absent father or mother who refuses to

154

make contact with his or her children is a heartbreaking one, but the parent who has custody does not have to give up the idea that contact is lost for good. A woman wrote to a national newspaper to describe the almost heroic efforts she made to spark some interest from her former husband in their two boys. For several years she sent Christmas cards from them, photographs, school reports and regular letters telling him how they were getting on. After silence for all this time, he began to reply and eventually started seeing the boys, taking them on outings and finally establishing a regular relationship with them.

All this is good reason for working persistently for some contact between a child and both parents. Where the absent parent is extremely difficult, there may be sound reasons to keep them away from the children. However, in less extreme cases, it can be argued that a child who meets the parent at least once in a while will see who and what they are and make up their own minds as they get older. Without being able to meet the absent parent a child may wonder themselves, as an adult, whether the parent they lived with was hopelessly biased about the other one. They are also less likely needlessly to idealise the parent they never knew.

If the relationship has deteriorated to the extent that you and your partner are incapable of meeting on reasonable terms, or where the absent parent is likely to abduct the child, it is still possible to maintain visits through one of the access centres operated by the Probation Service. Under this system, a Probation Service social worker meets the child and the parent who has custody at the centre, takes charge of the child and hands them over to the visiting parent in another room. Afterwards the social worker hands the child back. There is no need for the parents to meet if they do not want to.

Such visits are likely to be arranged for weekends, and toys and teamaking equipment are provided. It depends on individual circumstances whether or not the social worker remains present throughout the visit, but in some cases it is a way of providing practical support while the absent parent establishes their own relationship with the child. There are not many of these centres, but the Probation Service is able, in similar ways, to mediate so that parents can reach practical agreements about their children.

For most parents things do not become this traumatic, but nevertheless the natural difficulties of re-arranging lives to cope with divorce is rarely easy. If a difficult period can be overcome so that there is no longer any upset, it makes a big contribution to the children's security for them to see that their parents can still get on together despite living apart. More than this, both parents eventually may gain respect in the child's eyes much later for having cared enough to maintain the links, especially if the child compares their own situation with that of others.

One of the most difficult events to handle during the transition to a new life-style is Christmas—for it is then that parents and children feel most keenly the pangs which affect a divided family. The first Christmas after a family breaks up is often traumatic and can be a very uncomfortable time, because even parents who are on reasonable terms with each other are usually unsure whether they should have a family Christmas for the children's sake, or not. And the children are very likely to ask: "Is Daddy (or Mummy) coming to see us?" Christmas in most people's lives is an important time when family ties take centre stage, even in families which are not particularly close.

Many separated couples with children manage to arrange at least a meal or a brief time together as a family at the first Christmas after the break-up. Some are able to spend Christmas Day, or half of it, together and may even need the guarded warmth that this provides. Tactfully handled (and with an explanation to the children in advance that it is for Christmas only), it is an excellent chance to put aside the year's difficulties and give the children some of the family spirit they need. Later, new patterns for spending Christmas are created as both partners establish new lives. But it is important for children that Christmas continues to be marked by their parents acting together as far as they are capable in the circumstances, and even if it is impossible to meet. Ways of doing this include:

- Discuss and agree in good time whether the absent parent will visit.

- Make a proper arrangement about the time and duration.

- Decide jointly what presents the children should have so that they don't get presents they already have, or the same thing twice. Do this by letter if necessary.

- Tell the children what plans are being made.

- Warn other relatives of arrangements or arrange to see them on another day or later on Christmas Day.

Birthdays are as important to children as Christmas. Beyond the joy of the celebrations, the presents and the party, each birthday, to a child, is a turning point in the year which confirms that he or she is growing up. Children need their parents to share the occasion in some way, even a parent who rarely sees the child—it means so much. To send a card takes little effort but it shows more than anything else that you care, no matter what the circumstances.

In the process of overcoming the upset of separation and divorce, many people try to block out thoughts of the partner who has gone. However, children need to have the opportunity to talk and allow their feelings about the absent parent to be exposed. So it is important to resist the urge to suppress the subject with your children, if you feel this way, even if talking about it upsets you. Allow the child's hurt feelings and accept them. And accept your own hurt feelings too.

The legal arrangements which are made for the children in the divorce settlement are a key to both partners' future relationships with them. The majority of couples settle for custody being granted to one of them, usually the mother, with access given to the father. This means, in most cases, the person who has custody takes on the full-time responsibility for the children's daily care, and effectively brings them up alone. They will also take most, if not all, of the major decisions concerning the children—on education, serious medical matters, change of religion, consent to marry and so on. This is a considerable burden for one person to bear, perhaps for fifteen years or more, and particularly if they have several children to look after. This responsibility is not easy to share even if they live with someone or re-marry, because the new father can rarely have the same relationship with a child as the natural parent; and the absent parent still has a say, legally, in important decisions affecting the child.

Joint custody is a settlement which gives both parents a full and equal say in the major decisions. Its increasing use in this country shows a greater willingness by parents to continue to share the essential decision-making in their children's lives. One parent will still be declared by the court to have daily care and control but it lightens their load enormously to have the other parent actively concerned with the children's upbringing. More important, the children will be aware that the absent parent is still involved with them, because under this arrangement the parents are effectively working together for the children's benefit. This creates a very positive climate as the children grow up. However there are difficulties. It does demand application and persistence to make joint custody work, and sometimes keeps the telephone line busy. But tactfully handled, there need be no more friction or difficulty than if the parents were still married.

Solicitors generally are not interested in the idea of joint custody because they undervalue the continuing close involvement in the children's lives that this implies. Martin Richards, head of the Cambridge University Child Care and Development Group says: "We talk of custody being won or lost or being awarded to a parent like a prize at a school speech day. Sole custody involves a winner and a loser. Having custody of your child removed from you is hardly a way to encourage a divorced parent to continue to be involved in the life of a child. Courts should never do this without very good reason. Instead they should go out of their way to confirm the continuing role of both parents."*

The spirit of co-operation we are suggesting can be seen in action when it comes to children's schooling. It takes time but try to attend at least one or two of the important school

* *One Parent Times*, October 1981 (National Council for One Parent Families)

functions together, such as sports day and open days, and school plays. Children love to see their parents at such events—to catch a glimpse of them from the stage or running track—and for at least one to turn up is part of normal parenting. All children need the reassurance of their interest in them and it is especially important to children of divorced parents.

Schools nowadays are very well aware of difficulties that confront such children. Often secondary schools have a comprehensive pastoral care system set up to make sure that the general welfare of the children is looked after as much as the educational aspects. Teachers in primary schools often know the child's personal situation in detail and therefore can be sympathetic to any school problem. Schools find out about divorced families in several ways: through the parents themselves, as an outcome of a child's difficulties, or a child may mention it himself. In a comprehensive school we visited, one divorce a week is brought to the notice of the appropriate staff and the local Educational Welfare Officer often finds that the parents of a child who plays truant or is frequently absent, are divorced.

It is important for a school to know when there is separation or a divorce because this is a major change in circumstances, similar to other upheavals such as a house move or a death, which may affect school work and behaviour for a time. The school will also want to know which parent has custody so that it knows how to deal with parents over matters such as school notices, reports and fees. Where young children are concerned, the school may need this information in order to know which parent is supposed to collect the child at the end of the day, or whether it is a parent's wish, or court order, that the other parent should not meet the child. Try to be open with the school staff about the situation. Schools are usually glad that both parents are still involved and will normally send notices separately to each if asked.

The pressures on children at this time may be reflected in their health. Some children become susceptible to ailments such as sore throats, tummy cramps, earache, headache and skin rashes. Illnesses such as asthma may worsen or even develop at this time. These are, in effect, an outward expression of a child's attempt to deal with the emotional problems. At the comprehensive school we mentioned the Matron told us that most of the children whose illnesses she treated were linked with parents "who are together but in friction, or are separated". This again strongly suggests that parents who are separated or divorced should sort out their differences as far as they can, to lift the strain off their children.

One way in which children can be helped with more serious problems is through the various social agencies. At school, if there are work or behavioural problems, the educational welfare officer or child psychologist may be called in to help both school and parents find a way to maintain the child's progress. He or she can offer advice to ease the situation and may suggest one of a range of solutions.

Sometimes the problems involving the child may be too difficult for parents to handle without help. Family relationships are complex enough at the best of times but when the family is under pressure such as divorce the various inter-relationships themselves may be at the heart of the problems which are troubling the child. It is not a question of blame or feeling guilty, or of being a bad parent, but of trying to understand and change the underlying pattern which lies behind the difficulty. This complicated area of family life may be impossible to resolve without professional help. Organisations such as the child-guidance clinics—run by the health authorities—or family therapy centres like the Tavistock Clinic in London, and the Probation Service and Family Welfare Association counselling sessions, all provide a means of exploring and dealing with the issues involved.

The difficulties that younger children have in coping with their parents' divorce are often underestimated, since children find it hard to deal with their feelings. The pioneering scheme started in 1981 by Leicester Probation Service, in which they are seen in groups without their parents and encouraged to express their feelings through play, role-playing and discussion, recognises this fact. This is another facet of treating children as people in their own right and a method which deserves to become

/ more widespread.

Some people feel a sense of failure as a parent at the thought of needing to ask for professional help from agencies such as these, or are tempted to believe that the problem will go away of its own accord. Although it can sometimes happen, this loss of confidence is one of the many new situations you may meet and deal with in the complicated process of divorce, and you will have to judge for yourself the best course to take.

Children *can* survive these experiences and prosper in the life that lies ahead of them—if the right conditions are created. As Kahlil Gibran says: "Your children are not your children . . . but you may give them your love", and this is what will help them most.

CHAPTER 8

Parents, Relations and Friends

"I could tell you my adventures—beginning from this morning," said Alice a little timidly. "But it's no use going back to yesterday because I was a different person then"—*Alice's Adventures in Wonderland (Lewis Carroll)*

The essential meaning of "The Family" changes when you separate and divorce, so that new patterns of living have to be found. Similarly your relationship to friends will alter too, and new priorities present themselves. This chapter is about the various shifts and changes which can occur and how to cope with them. It is also about the help and opportunities which can present themselves when you very much need them. At this time nearly everyone needs the lifeline that the network of family and friends provide. With a positive attitude, this period can lead to a new equilibrium, a time when you are able to strike out in the world again.

Parents are hit hard by the break-up of their children's marriages and the initial separation is often a severe shock. Older people usually have their own attitudes towards marriage and the pressures involved, and they may not easily understand what you are going through and the reasons for the breakdown. Often their reaction to the breakdown of a marriage which has seemed secure is one of saying: "They had such a lovely home together, and lovely children. I cannot understand why he (or she) wanted to leave." This comment can be a reflection of the difficulties in communication between parents and their married son or daughter. If parents and child have been unable to discuss their feelings together, then the parents will not have the knowledge to understand, though this can be developed. Time itself can help.

Disappointment and resignation are natural and understandable reactions when parents hear about the break-up. Because the promise of a lifetime's commitment has been broken, they can easily feel responsible in some way rather than look at your particular situation as it is. They may have a sound and happy marriage themselves which has survived the difficult times and wonder, therefore, where they "went wrong".

Often parents do notice difficulties and ask about them at an earlier stage. When you have frequent contact with your parents they are more likely already to be aware of changes in the marriage. If you have a good relationship with them, these may be the first people you turn to. If they live at a distance or you rarely contact each other, then you can choose more easily the point at which you say anything—or indeed you may be asked. This could be the first time you share your smouldering feelings with someone else and it can be important for you to fully acknowledge them.

Parents can be supportive or perplexed, or both, but the way you discuss the subject and what you say will depend very much on how you get on with them. It may be necessary to consider what they are able to handle, especially for example if a parent is ill, or rigid in their views. You may have to choose whether to say anything at all or to postpone talking to them for a long time.

Some parents find it difficult to offer support and become angry or resort to blame as a way of coping with the situation. This is something to try to sidestep as far as possible since it is destructive and probably merely a replay of their attitudes towards you as a child and young adult. The urge to blame can lead parents to take sides, sometimes even feeling less sympathetic to their son or daughter than to the person they married. Alternatively, parents may side with their own children and see them as blameless. You may have to cope with such attitudes, to stand up for yourself and put your own point of view.

There are good reasons for doing this. Firstly, it is a matter of your own self-respect, and secondly, if you have children, you have a responsibility to protect them from family disagreements about the marriage which will upset and confuse them. For example, should your parents strongly disapprove of your partner and take sides by strongly criticising him or her openly in front of the children, you will need to stop this by pointing out that the children will suffer and become insecure. By appealing to their better nature as grandparents, it is possible to persuade them to be more careful about the remarks they make; it is better still to persuade them not to discuss the subject when the children are around. If this does not work and you feel the children are hearing things you do not want them to, you might have to alter the pattern of contact. One way is to try to make sure you are with the children when they meet their grandparents. Another is to limit the grandparents' contact until things change.

Blame, anger and other unsympathetic reactions can stem from hidden feelings of which parents are unaware. They may be angry with themselves for having "failed" as parents. Outbursts can also mask underlying resentment where one parent, or even both, wanted to leave their own marriage in the past but never did. A parent might even confide that they wish they had left, and this can lead to some understanding between you. Or it may simply be that they cannot understand what is going on and the reasons why.

Marriage break-up often brings back to the surface the intimate relationship between parents and their children which was apparently discarded by the time of the marriage. A man or woman, facing life alone, can find themselves the "child" once more in their relationship with their parents—at the stage it was when they originally left home. This can happen at any time in adulthood so that even a person in their thirties or forties with children of their own may be treated as if they were still a teenager or a small child. The support and practical help parents provide when a marriage breaks down will usually be welcome, even badly needed, but it is worth being aware that there are dangers for some families. You could find your own personality, or certain parts of it, reflected like a mirror or brought up again. If this happens, the positive side is the opportunity to become aware and gain insights into undeveloped parts of yourself and so make changes. One unfortunate result can be that someone who is badly hurt emotionally can return permanently to a childlike relationship with their parents, even moving back in with them for good, particularly if they didn't lead an independent life before they married. If nothing else, someone who, for example, has gone straight from home into marriage, gains a lot of independence if they become separated and this is not something which should be given up in a hurry.

The relationship you have had with your parents up to now is the starting point for talking with them about your life and what you are going to do. Many people find this is not easy for a variety of reasons, and this is particularly so where there has been a fraught relationship for some years. Even in caring families you may quickly need to establish an adult-to-adult relationship. This helps to prevent an adult-child pattern re-establishing itself, and it could prevent the relationship deteriorating. Be prepared to talk to them. Parents often have more maturity and understanding of life than we allow, even when, perhaps because of age or their own circumstances, there is little they can actually do. Their help can come in other ways. One mother in her seventies wrote a concerned but reassuring letter to a daughter leaving her marriage after twenty years saying: "I hope you find peace of mind."

Those who cannot turn to a parent may instead be close to an uncle, aunt, cousin or grandparent in whom they can confide. Indeed, this may be someone they have been close to since childhood. Since in many ways they provide the function of a parent, they can offer similar help but perhaps with a little more detachment. Many a family has a wise relative, perhaps an elderly uncle or aunt, who has seen much in a long life and provides a calming influence—often saying just what is needed, like the mother mentioned above.

A brother or sister, usually someone of your own age group, can provide a different kind of support. You may be fortunate that their views and values of life are broadly like yours, so they can easily sympathise. Perhaps they have gone through a similar experience themselves or, like a friend, are simply calm and steady when you are feeling otherwise. They may be sufficiently detached to point out some things you may not want to hear. This kind of honesty is not always welcome but sometimes you can learn from it.

Separation and divorce can easily lead to divisions which

exclude our in-laws. It can seem "right" and "normal" that with separation, the relationship with our partner's family should also cease. Though things may change, there is no reason, unless you have to, to cut off valid relationships that have been built up over a number of years. Indeed, it would be artificial and even hurtful to do so. Parents-in-law or other relatives on your partner's side may value your relationship with them more than you realise. One woman whose parents-in-law knew how badly their son had treated her, gave her every support when he went off with someone else. Later, after a divorce, she was asked by her former husband's sister to be a godparent to the sister's new baby. Though this relationship continued, some do have to be let go and sometimes circumstances prevent you from doing otherwise. It is a difficult area in which you may need to judge for yourself. Trust your instincts.

The point at which a couple separate marks for most of them the beginning of a shakeup in their friendships. New friends may emerge, longstanding ones can disappear and some relationships change in character. On top of everything else you find the need to make different adjustments among your circle of friends. It is a time when true friends show themselves and new ones help to shape your future life.

This re-mix of friends can seem very random but we are convinced it has a purpose: there must now be a profound change that reflects new areas of involvement in your life. There is no predicting what these might be but you must remain open to them. In fact, this book had its origins in a chance meeting at a party between two men who were re-establishing their social life during the period surrounding separation and divorce.

Marriage can be like a time capsule because its demands take up so much of our time and most of us expect the structure of marriage to provide so many of our emotional needs; friendships have to be fitted into the time that is left. For these reasons many people feel very vulnerable when they find themselves establishing social contacts as a single person again. It can be difficult enough if you are in your twenties or early thirties and married for several years. For someone in their fifties who has been married for twenty-five years or more it can seem an overwhelming problem. Yet people do meet the challenge at this age and beyond it, sometimes establishing a lively social life of a kind not possible for them thirty years earlier.

As an individual you now have to create your own structure of friendships so it is no wonder that you may feel awkward and vulnerable at first: it can be like coming out of a tunnel into daylight. This vulnerability is mixed with bewilderment, even shock sometimes, when you find yourself having to revalue your existing friendships and evaluate new ones at the same time as you are re-assessing yourself. This transformation becomes more acute for the older person who may have lived to a set pattern for many years and is now trying to cope with a completely different lifestyle. If you find yourself crying, allow it as a welcome release!

Women are generally more adept than men at making lasting friendships at an emotional level, as well as making a deeper commitment to marriage. Most men, on the other hand, find it difficult to share their feelings and their friendships tend to be based on work or spare time interests rather than friendship itself. Consequently, a woman will be strongly sustained by her women friends when a marriage breaks up, while a man is unlikely to receive this support from his male friends, though he has some protection in his greater concern with work and the outside world.

Most people have staunch friends who will always stand by them, but within established friendships some people fade out of your life and others become more important. Some of your friends may feel vulnerable too. Your separation and divorce provokes some unspoken thoughts in couples that you know. These can be concerns about sensitive areas of their own relationships which even result in your being rejected by them. Another reason for rejection is that they may feel embarrassed and would like to help but do not know how to. Equally, they may not be able to relate to you as a single person instead of half a couple, or they could have taken sides and kept their sympathies for your partner.

So many of us are inclined to act in set ways and all kinds of attitudes and judgments can come into play. For example, the assumption by the female partner that a divorced woman on her own, when invited to a meal, is a threat to her relationship, is reckoned to be a common one. This feeling of threat often leads to rejection of the woman which can be very hurtful. In contrast, a divorced man on his own is often thought of, again by the female partner, as someone who needs a good meal and is therefore a welcome guest. This could be a reflection of a number of aspects in the man–woman relationship stemming from old roles and assumptions. Perhaps women often sense their man has less emotional commitment to their relationship than they have, and that he might easily be tempted. There may be an unjustified assumption by both that the single woman could be interested in the man when all she really wants is the meal and the company—as does the man.

To feel yourself rejected by friends when you may be low anyway and facing other problems is painful. If you want to stay good friends don't let the opportunity pass to ask directly what is bothering them underneath. Are they judging you without knowing the full story? Are they just angry or upset for some reason? Or are you behaving in a manner likely to put them off so that they don't want your company? The answer may be simpler than you realise since they may be in a serious dilemma: do they stay friends with you, with your separated partner, or both? This raises the problem for them of whether to invite you to visit, or your ex-partner. They may even cope with the dilemma by cutting you both off for a while, or for good. If you feel yourself cut off in this way regard it, perhaps, as a necessary part of the change in your pattern of friendships. Some friends, inevitably, will drift away but others will take their place if you allow it. One of the big problems here is that the rejection of friends, added perhaps to that of your partner, can build up a pattern of expecting things to turn out badly. When you continually think this, life itself will tend to treat you accordingly.

New friends that you make can help you look on the bright side but you also have to look towards the bright side to make them. People are prepared to make the effort with someone who is going through a difficult experience provided they feel you are moving forward, however slowly. New friends can introduce you to areas of experience you might not have explored before. They act as catalysts. Simply through knowing them you can discover and involve yourself in interests and activities not attempted before.

Some of these friendships may be passing ones, lasting only a few weeks or months, or even a day or two. Do not under-rate them. You may find yourself sharing thoughts and ideas with someone even for an hour which you realise at the time, or later, are important for you. Some of these ideas which could have been at the back of your mind for a long time now begin to crystallise. Experiences too come up unexpectedly and can be significant, if you are open to them. These passing friends and experiences are all part of developing and changing into a more mature person. You could easily find that by meeting and relating to new people you recognise and learn about "unused" parts of yourself. It is events like these that make people say: "Talking to him struck a chord in me" or "Being with her drew me out".

This can be a remarkable period of consolidation at a personal level. It helps us to recognise that we are incomplete in many ways and yet life's experiences and the people we meet have much to teach us. The question is: are we prepared to learn? Life at times is like a jigsaw puzzle in which the pieces are mixed up and have to be rearranged into a new picture. It becomes a task and responsibility to do this for yourself and overcome the various emotional and practical difficulties you find yourself in A strange kind of freedom now appears no matter what your circumstances: without marriage, time takes on a different meaning. You are presented with choices of what to do with your time. Patterns change. At one extreme you may want to withdraw and stay at home night after night. At the other you may go out every night and fill all your spare time by socialising. Either way you may feel very much alone and even the freedom to do what you want may not dispel this state of mind. You have potentially the emotional freedom and perhaps the physical freedom to do as you please. We acknowledge the practical difficulties in finding a new lifestyle, particularly for a mother or father tied to the home and children. Remember that some kind of balance that keeps a thread of normal activities going will be a stabilising influence. Nevertheless, to turn some of your energy towards a new life will help create it.

Separation and divorce is one of life's crises in which an opportunity is given to build up increasing confidence in who you are and what you want to do. Those who can accept the past and meet the challenge of the future talk of having an increasing sense of completeness. This embraces an awareness of what they need and want in life together with the development of those qualities which have not been fully expressed. This can bring a new kind of tolerance, sensitivity and caring, and equally a firmness in dealing with people born of an increasing strength within. These are some of the other sides of ourselves we have to find. It is part of the process we have talked about throughout the book, a stage in the journey that is life itself.

Conclusions

A social worker and divorce counsellor, Betty Rubinstein, describes the older generation's failure to prepare people for the realities of marriage as: "Like launching a ship without lifeboats although it is known there are rocks ahead."* We can only agree. Parents and other relatives are often unaware of the skills they could be passing on to enable future conflict to be faced and resolved where possible.

We have tried to show that the skills required to go through marital breakdown with the minimum of bitterness can be learned. It is likely to be some time in the future before widespread fear and lack of knowledge can be overcome to the extent that it will be more usual for people to arrange their divorces with care, consideration and compassion.

This area is made more difficult by the degree to which roles can take us over. We learn them from many sources, including our families. More obvious, though, is the relentless exposure of behaviour stereotypes in the media; men being shown frequently as active, aggressive and often violent, and women as passive and decorative. It is true this is changing now with films and television, for example, showing more women as independent and able to take care of themselves—while men at last can be shown to have feelings. Nevertheless, women are still being portrayed as mindless in a way that seldom applies to men. Think of soap powder commercials. We believe that such advertising, which undermines women's confidence in themselves by devaluing them, makes its own contribution to relationship difficulties.

A more direct encouragement of stereotyped roles in marriage is found in the British Medical Association's widely distributed advice booklet, *Getting Married*. This well-meaning publication does offer helpful advice, such as being "honest about our emotions" and warning that: "Perhaps both men and

* *New Law Journal*, November 4, 1983

women tend to view marriage through rose-coloured spectacles without accepting that, like anything else, it needs working at."

However, even this is presented in the context of a constant bombardment of traditional images and a patronising tone which speak louder than the text. The booklet is heavily consumer-oriented with illustrations which are used to sell furniture and other goods, and captions that list the prices. A double message is being given of offering sensible advice in the context of sheer consumerism, which puts a smokescreen across the realities of marriage relationships.

These two examples are visible signs of many pressures and confusions about marriage and divorce. Feminists and progressive women's magazines have laboured for years to reject enslaving images of this kind, to the benefit of both sexes. But men have a lot of catching up to do. They have no equivalent press which, through the use of simplified psychology, can help them see themselves independently of the roles they are expected to fulfil. There is a shift men need to make in awareness of their own individuality instead of merely feeling defensive.

We have mentioned the problems of women a great deal in this book, with good reason. Their particular burdens in marriage—often added to by their husbands' limited view of women in general—are a key to many of the difficulties which lead to divorce. One question which we believe is worth some consideration is this: To what extent is the development of a woman's sense of identity affected by taking her husband's name when they marry, and how much does this add to the feelings involved in marriage break-up? We suggest that to change names on marriage, though not legally required, is not the simple act that it seems and could have deeper implications which are not fully understood.

Marriage is one of the rare occasions when the Church comes directly into people's lives. Yet it can be argued that the Anglican and Roman Catholic churches could explain more publicly the nature of marriage and what it entails. The churches could, for example, publish a comprehensive and widely available booklet covering the obligations of marriage, including the legal ones. This type of booklet needs to be on sale to the general public and could be used as a basis for work in schools.

The Church of England's reluctant decision, in November 1983, to allow remarriage in church on the basis of an inquiry into each case, revealed a dilemma between its theology and the realities of divorce in everyday life. If the Church is prepared to invest time and thought in rigorous examination of the motives behind second marriage, and the suitability of people to enter into it, why does it not apply a similar test to people marrying for the first time?

People marry for many reasons but while they are asked to be true to each other, they need equally to be true to themselves. They do make mistakes, immature decisions or grow away from their partners, and complications in individual sexuality can arise. In such circumstances the vow to live together until death is perhaps unrealistic.

The churches have to find ways of reconciling their attitudes to marriage and divorce with their doctrine of forgiveness.

Schools still have a long way to go in teaching children how to empathise and relate to others. Drama is often used for this purpose but communication of this kind could be taught widely as a specific subject. Perhaps a fourth R should be added to the three R's, which are now called "basic skills". Surely the fourth basic skill is Relationship. Knowing how to relate is as important in leading your life as being literate and numerate.

Another area in which schools have to progress is making sure that sexual discrimination and role stereotyping is finally rooted out. Vigorous efforts have been made in the last decade but there are still many inappropriate books on the shelves of primary schools. Some children continue to learn from texts and illustrations which show boys climbing trees or helping Dad while girls stand and watch or help Mum. This may seem less important than learning to read, until it is realised that children will, to a large extent, base their own relationships on these early images and the assumptions which go with them.

Unfortunately, the restrictions on education spending make it extremely difficult for schools to replace these books with more suitable non-sexist publications. If the government wants sex-equality legislation to be fully effective its priority must be in education and it must allocate its resources accordingly.

The vital part that solicitors play in many divorces raises the question of whether the training they receive for this work is appropriate. Family law is only part of a very full course. There is little opportunity for trainee solicitors to consider aspects such as achieving empathy with clients, and how to reduce acrimony. Whether or not solicitors learn ways to be constructive and caring, as well as to deal efficiently with legal problems is dependent on the personality and approach of individual lecturers. It would be of immense benefit to divorce proceedings if the teaching of family law had a stronger counselling component enabling all solicitors to offer their clients understanding and reassurance.

The establishment of the Solicitors' Family Law Association, with its conciliatory approach to divorce work, is an excellent step forward. Its courses help to share and develop the skills of divorce solicitors.

The gradual spread of divorce conciliation services, as Michael Simmons argues, can make the solicitor's job easier by working in parallel with clients and taking some of the "social work" load from him. He says: "No solicitor should feel threatened if his client seeks help from a conciliation agency... In fact I will go further and suggest that the solicitor ought to be active in referring his client to such an agency with whom he knows he can work happily... Mutual exchanges of ideas often produce solutions to the problems, which the solicitor on his own might not have reached."*

The work of the conciliation agencies is likely to become increasingly important in the years ahead. At the moment it is an embryo service, pioneered in Bristol and offered in various towns by groups of people drawn from the helping agencies. The Government, unwisely, has rejected the idea of a state service but fortunately it looks as if a national service is on the way under the aegis of the National Divorce and Conciliation Service, which is setting standards and acting as the co-ordinating body.

* *Law Society Gazette*, January 26, 1983

Legislation in all areas tends to reflect social change. The recent moves to change the 1969 divorce laws to make the interests of children the first priority and to help both partners become self-sufficient, are sound principles for divorce in the 1980s. Children's interests must be of at least equal priority with those of their parents in both the emotional and financial aspects. The new legislation is designed to make sure that this is so. It also acknowledges the very fundamental point that two people who divorce have to accept that they cannot be in the same financial position afterwards. This at last recognises an important reality which people have found hard to admit. The uncertainty that this has generated about the possible impact on the welfare of families is a real one. Safeguards are necessary, but beyond the rules of authority is the wider issue of personal responsibility, both within marriage and when a marriage ends. This book has been arguing for greater individual responsibility in relationships and the new legislation may encourage more people to look at things in this way.

As with any laws on divorce, the new legislation must be interpreted with care, but it does provide a framework for people to lead independent lives in the future. To divorce is not only a matter of facing the practical, emotional and legal problems, but of recognising the inner psychological world which lies behind the marriage relationships we seek and which many of us end. This inner world is a reality which cannot be ignored.

Explanation of Various Legal Terms and Procedures

Here is a list of words and special phrases used in divorce proceedings. It helps to make yourself familiar with them.

Access — The arrangements made by parents and the courts for children to see the parent they are not living with. This includes collecting children for the day, outings, having them for the weekend or taking them on holiday.

Acknowledgement of Service — The form sent with the initial divorce papers (the petition) which asks whether the partner intends to oppose the divorce or not.

Affidavit — Form completed by the person applying for a divorce (petitioner) which confirms, an oath that the information given in the petition is correct.

Ancillary Relief — This covers the financial or property settlement orders made by the court as part of the divorce arrangements. These can be settled in advance by two partners, or decided by the court at the time.

Answer — A reply in which a partner denies allegations that are made in the divorce petition. This can be set out in a letter.

Application — A document from either partner asking for the court to make various orders; for example for access, custody, variations of maintenance or an injunction to limit the other person's actions in some way.

Care and Control — Court order assigning the everyday care of children, usually granted to the parent with whom the children live or will live.

Conciliation — The process in which a mediator helps a couple resolve issues in dispute before their divorce hearing.

Co-respondent	The person named in a divorce proceeding as having committed adultery with one of the partners.
Courts	There are two kinds of courts which deal with divorce in England and Wales: a Divorce County Court for all unopposed cases and the High Court for opposed cases. Cases which start as unopposed cases in a Divorce County Court and become opposed are transferred to the High Court.
Cross Petition	A statement in which the partner answering the divorce petition seeks a divorce for reasons of his or her own.
Custody	A court order for one parent to be responsible for all the major decisions in the children's upbringing, for example schooling, medical and surgical decisions, consent to marry and choice of religion. In practice both parents may decide these together, or if there is a dispute the non-custodial parent can apply to the court to make their views known on a particular issue.
Joint Custody	A court order that automatically enables both parents to share the important decisions about their children's upbringing.
Decree Nisi	The provisional granting by the court of a divorce which is made final six weeks later provided the court is satisfied about arrangements for the children and any other matters, e.g. that the partners have not been reconciled.
Decree Absolute	The final granting of a divorce which makes it permanent. This frees you to re-marry.
Direction for Trial	The order made by the court to go ahead with the divorce hearing after receiving a request from the petitioner or his/her solicitor.
Equity	The value of a house or other assets, or the money available once they are sold after the amount due on a mortgage and all costs have been deducted.

Exhibit	A document such as a signed statement sent with the affidavit to give further information.
Filing	The process of lodging documents with the court for rubber stamping and service to other parties. This validates the documents.
Financial Provision Order	Ruling by the court to allocate a family's finances as part of ancillary relief. It may take the form of maintenance, a lump sum payment, transfer of property, settlements on children.
Green Form	Government scheme to provide subsidised work by a solicitor for an uncomplicated divorce. This is available to people on low incomes and limited capital.
In Chambers	The private hearing by a judge of the divorce arrangements, very often concerning how children will be looked after, where they will live, or go to school.
Injunction	A court order limiting the actions of a partner to protect the other partner. This can be quite specific, for example preventing someone from molesting their partner or coming within a certain distance of the family home. It can also turn an offending partner out of the home (then called an "Ouster Injunction"). Penalty for breaking the order can be imprisonment.
Judicial Separation	Procedure enabling a couple to use the court to make their separation official but not to divorce them. The court has the same wide powers as in making divorce orders to grant settlements on children, money and property. Particularly used by people who do not agree with divorce.
Legal Aid	Scheme administered by the Law Society to provide the cost of legal work where there are matters in dispute which have to go to court. However the costs may have to be paid by one or other of the partners and this can take the form of a charge over any property or other assets.
Maintenance Order	The regular weekly or monthly payments a court orders one partner to pay the other for support of herself (or himself) and children.

Next Friend

An adult who acts in court on behalf of a child. This may be a parent who has custody, a legal guardian or social worker.

Nullity

A decree granted by the court to end a marriage which is ruled invalid, for example if one of the partners was already married to someone else (bigamy) or a marriage has not been consummated. The court has the same powers to make financial provisions as in a valid marriage.

Party Cited

The person named by the respondent to have committed adultery with the petitioner.

Petition

These are the papers which initiate divorce. They are lodged with the court by the person seeking the divorce (the petitioner) or by their solicitor. The court sends a copy to the partner (the respondent).

Petitioner

The person who starts divorce proceedings by filing a petition with the court.

Periodical Payments Order

A maintenance order.

Property Adjustment Order

Ruling by the court to divide a family's capital assets such as a house—a part of ancillary relief.

Reconciliation

The getting together again of a couple during or after divorce proceedings.

Registrar

The court official who examines the divorce application and attends to all preliminary steps such as fixing a date for the hearing and who also deals with most Ancillary Relief applications.

Respondent

The partner against whom the divorce action is brought.

Sealing

Official stamping of documents filed at the court and of orders and decrees.

Service

The arrangement to give documents such as petitions and decrees to the parties for whom they are intended. This can be by post or handing them over personally.

Small Maintenance Payments

Maintenance orders of not more than £33 a week or £143 a month to a partner or to children for whom the payments are made in full without tax deduction.

Void Marriage/
Voidable Marriage

Terms used to describe invalid marriages. Void marriage is one that is ruled to be non-existent, as in bigamy. Voidable marriage is a legal union which has failed to be an actual marriage for reasons such as lack of consummation and unfitness for marriage. Reasons can include marriage under duress or where a partner is suffering from a statutory mental disorder when they marry.

Organisations

These addresses were up-to-date at the time of going to Press. Some of them are central offices which will give details of local centres.

Children's Legal Centre,
20, Compton Terrace,
London, N1 2UN
Tel: 01-359-6251 (Telephone advice service 2–5pm)

Citizens Advice Bureau,—
(National Association of Citizens Advice Bureaux)
110, Drury Lane,
London WC2B 5SW
Tel: 01-836-9231

Family Rights Group,
6–9, Manor Gardens,
Holloway Road,
London, N7 6LA
Tel: 01-272-4231

Family Crisis Counselling Service,
Bishop Creighton House,
Lillie Road,
London SW6
Tel: 01-385-8400

Gingerbread,
35, Wellington Street,
London, WC2E 7BN
Tel: 01-240-0953/4

Institute of Marital Studies,
Tavistock Centre,
120, Belsize Lane,
London, NW3 5BA
Tel: 01-435-7111

Institute of Family Therapy (London),
43, New Cavendish Street,
London, WIM 7RG
Tel: 01-935-1651

The Jewish Marriage Education Council,
529b, Finchley Road,
London, NW3 7BG
Tel: 01-794-5222

London Youth Advisory Centre,
26, Prince of Wales Road,
Kentish Town,
London, NW5 3LG
Tel: 01-267-4792

National Council for One Parent Families,
255, Kentish Town Road,
London, NW5 2LX
Tel: 01-267-1361

National Society for the Prevention of Cruelty to Children,
1, Riding House,
London, W1
Tel: 01-580-8812

Organisation for Parents Under Stress (OPUS),
26, Manor Drive,
Pickering,
N. Yorkshire, YO18 8DD
Tel: 0751-73235

Parents Anonymous,
6–9, Manor Gardens,
London, N7 6LA
Tel: 01-263-8918

National Marriage Guidance
   Council,
Herbert Gray College,
Little Church Street,
Rugby, CV21 3AP
Tel: 0788-73241

Scottish Marriage Guidance
   Council,
26, Frederick Street,
Edinburgh, EH2 2JR
Tel: 031-225-5006

The Catholic Marriage Advisory
   Council,
15, Lansdowne Road,
Holland Park,
London, W11 3AJ
Tel: 01-727-0141/2

Divorce Conciliation and Advisory
   Service,
38, Ebury Street,
London, SW1 0LU
Tel: 01-730-2422

Families Need Fathers,
Elfrida Hall,
Campshill Road,
London, SE13
Tel: 01-852-7123

Campaign for Justice in Divorce,
PO Box 9,
Hereford, HR1 3UT
Tel: 0423-79308

Child Poverty Action Group,
1, Macklin Street,
London, WC2
Tel: 01-242-9149

The National Council for the
   Divorced and Separated,
13, High Street,
Little Shelford,
Cambs. CB2 5ES
Tel: 0923-22181

The National Family Conciliation
   Council,
155, High Street,
Dorking,
Surrey, RH4 1AD
Tel: Dorking 882754

Problems with Step-Children,
June Mason,
9, Cottage Lane,
Chasetown,
Nr. Walsall, WS7 8XZ
Tel: 054-36-76910

National Step-Family Association,
Maris House,
Maris Lane,
Trumpington,
Cambridge, CB2 2LB
Tel: 0223-841306

Shelter, The National Campaign
   for the Homeless,
157, Waterloo Road,
London, SE1 8XF
Tel: 01-633-9377

Solicitors Family Law Association,
c/o 154, Fleet Street,
London, EC4A 2HX
Tel: 01-353-3290

Mothers Apart from their Children
   (MATCH)
64, Delaware Mansions,
Delaware Road,
London, W9

Family Welfare Association,
Central Office,
501–5, Kingsland Road,
London, E8 4AV
Tel: 01-254-6251
Also at: Milton Keynes 0908-678237
     Northampton 0104-409600

Women's Aid Federation, England
   (WAFE)
374, Gray's Inn Road,
London, WC1X 8BB

Welsh Women's Aid,
Incentive House,
Adam Street,
Cardiff
Tel: 0222-462291

Scottish Women's Aid,
11, St. Colmen Street,
Edinburgh.
Tel: 031-2258011

Northern Ireland Women's Aid,
143A, University Street,
Belfast 7
Tel: 0232-249041

Westminster Pastoral Foundation,
23, Kensington Square,
London, W8
Tel: 01-937-695

College of Psychic Studies,
16, Queensbury Place,
London, SW7 2EB

Gay Switchboard,
Tel: 01-837-7324
(Also, SIGMA, organisation for
   heterosexual partners where the
   other is gay—same Tel. No.)

Post Offices— Hold the addresses
   of statutory organisations such as
   the DHSS but the reference
   section of your local library
   should have a more
   comprehensive list of
   organisations.

Books to Read

There are a number of useful books which are of direct help to anyone finding themselves in marriage difficulties. We list some of them below:

Relationships

The Art of Loving, Erich Fromm (Unwin Paperbacks, 1975)
Don't Say Yes When You Want To Say No, Herbert Fensterheim and Jean Baer (Futura, 1976)
I'm O.K., You're O.K., Thomas A. Harris (Pan Books, 1973)
Marriage Crumble and How to Avoid It, Hazel Evans (Family Circle, 1979)
Marriage, Faith and Love, Jack Dominian (Darton, Longman and Todd, 1981)
Open Marriage, A new lifestyle for couples, Nena O'Neill and George O'Neill (Peter Owen, 1973)
Relating, An astrological guide to living with others on a small planet, Liz Greene (Coventure, 1978)
Your Erroneous Zones, Wayne W. Dyer (Sphere, 1977)

About Divorce

Breaking Up, A practical guide to separation, divorce and coping on your own, Rosemary Simon (Arrow, 1974)
Conciliation and Divorce, Judge Brian Grant (Barry Rose Publications, 1981)
Divorce, The things you thought you'd never need to know, Jill M. Black (Elliott Right Way Books, 1982)
On Getting Divorced, (Consumers' Association, 1979)
I'm Leaving, How to cope with the emotional problems of divorce, Bente and Gunnar Oberg (Jill Norman and Hobhouse, 1982)

Single Parents, A comprehensive and compassionate guide for the divorced, separated and the unmarried, Derek Bowskill (Futura, 1980)
Surviving the Breakup, How children and parents cope with divorce, Judith Wallerstein and Joan B. Kelly (Grant McIntyre, 1980)
Undefended Divorce, A guide for the petitioner acting without a solicitor (Lord Chancellor's Office, 1977)

On Men and Women

Everyman, A guide to men's bodies, needs and emotions, Derek Llewellyn-Jones (Oxford Paperback, 1981)
Everywoman, A gynaecological guide for life, Derek Llewellyn-Jones (Faber Paperbacks, 1972)
He, Understanding masculine psychology, Robert A. Johnson (Perennial Library, Harper & Row, 1977)
The Inner World of Choice, Frances G. Wickes (Coventure, 1977)
Knowing Woman, Irene Castillejo (Harper Colophon Books, 1973)
The Limits of Masculinity, Andrew Tolson (Tavistock, 1977)
The Moon and the Virgin, Nor Hall (Women's Press, 1980)
She, Understanding feminine psychology, Robert A. Johnson (Perennial Library, Harper & Row, 1977)
Stand Your Ground, A woman's guide to self-preservation, Kaleghl Quinn (Orbis Publishing 1983)
The Way of All Women, M. Esther Harding (Rider, 1971)
Woman's Mysteries, A psychological interpretation of the feminine principle as portrayed in myth, story and dreams, M. Esther Harding (Rider, 1982)

Children

Divorce and Your Children, Anne Hooper (Allen & Unwin, 1981)
Divorce Can Happen to the Nicest People, Peter Mayle (W.H. Allen, 1979)

The Inner World of Childhood, Frances G. Wickes (Coventure, 1977)
Saturday Parent, How to remain a parent in more than name, Peter Rowlands (Allen & Unwin, 1980)
We Don't All Live with Mum and Dad, (National Council for One Parent Families, 1982)
When Parents Split Up, Ann K. Mitchell (Macdonald, 1983)

Health

Alternative Medicine, Andrew Stanway (Penguin, 1982)
The Essential Psychotherapies, Theory and practice by the masters (Mentor, New American Library, 1982)
Our Bodies, Ourselves, A health book by and for women, Boston Women's Health Collective (Penguin, 1978)
Overcoming Depression, Paul Hauck (Sheldon Press, 1974)
Taking the Strain, Robert Eagle (BBC Publications, 1981)
The Alternative Health Guide, The first comprehensive consumer's guide to the choice in medical treatment for both minor and major ailments, Brian Inglis and Ruth West (Michael Joseph, 1983)

Bibliography

A Better Way Out, (The Law Society, 1979)

Children and Divorce, Report of an ecumenical working party on the effects of divorce on children (Church of England Children's Society, 1983)

The Farther Reaches of Human Nature, Abraham Maslow (Pelican, 1973)

The Female Eunuch, Germaine Greer (Panther, 1972)

The Feminine Mystique, Betty Friedan (Penguin, 1965)

The Finer Report, Report of the committee on one-parent families (Stationery Office, 1975)

Getting Married, (British Medical Association, 1983)

The I and the Not I, M. Esther Harding (Coventure, 1977)

A Job For Life, Discussion paper by National Children's Bureau, 1982)

Jung, His Life and Work, Barbara Hanna (Aldus Books, 1964 and Capricorn Books N.Y., 1976)

The Life and Work of Sigmund Freud, Ernest Jones (Pelican, 1964)

Man and His Symbols, ed. by Carl G. Jung and M.L. von Franz (Aldus Books, 1974)

Marital Breakdown, Jack Dominian (Penguin, 1968)

Marriage and the Standing Committee's Task. The Standing Committee's response to the motion, carried by the General Synod in July, 1981 requesting a report setting out a range of procedures for cases where it is appropriate for a divorced person to marry in church during the lifetime of a former partner (Central Board of the Church of England, 1983)

Marriage Matters, Consultative document by the Working Party on Marriage Guidance set up by the Home Office in consultation with the Department of Health and Social Security (HMSO, 1979)

Matrimonial Causes Procedure Committee, Consultation Paper, Mrs Judith Booth chairman (Lord Chancellor's Office September, 1983)

The MsTaken Body, Jeannette Kupfermann (Paladin Granada, 1981)

Nunaga, Ten years of Eskimo life, Duncan Pryde (Corgi, 1972)

Postnatal Depression, Vivienne Welburn (Fontana, 1980)

The Psychology of C.G. Jung, Jolande Jacobi (Routledge Paperback, 1981)

Puer Aeternus, Marie-Louise von Franz (Sigo Press, 1970)

Report of the Inter-departmental Committee on Conciliation (HMSO July 1983)

Saturn, A new look at an old devil, Liz Greene (Aquarian Press, 1980)

The Second Stage, Betty Friedan (Michael Joseph, 1982)

The Secret of Staying in Love, John Powell (Argus Communications, 1974)

What is to be done about the Family?, ed. Lynne Segal (Penguin, 1983)

What is to be done about Violence to Women?, Elizabeth Wilson (Penguin, 1983)

What Society Does to Girls, Joyce Nicholson (Virago, 1977)

Women Confined, Ann Oakley (Martin Robertson, 1980)

Index